BREAKING GROUND

Laying the foundations for success
in the construction industry:
the guide to managing money,
accountancy and tax

Copyright © 2017 Jeffrey Lermer and Karen Wyrwas

First published in 2017 by Fatal Black Publishing

42 Lytton Rd, New Barnet, Barnet EN5 5BY

www.lermer.co.uk

Every effort has been made to ensure that website addresses are correct at time of going to press. The publisher cannot be held responsible for the content of any website mentioned in this book.

All rights reserved. No part of this publication may be reproduced or transmitted in any form or by any means, electronic or mechanical, including photocopying and recording, or held within any information storage and retrieval system, without permission in writing from the publisher or under licence from the Copyright Licensing Agency Limited. Further details of such licences (for reprographic reproduction) may be obtained from the Copyright Licensing Agency Limited, Barnard's Inn, 86 Fetter Lane, London EC4A 1EN.

The rights of Jeffrey Lermer and Karen Wyrwas to be identified as the authors of this work have been asserted by them in accordance with the Copyright, Design and Patents Act 1998.

Cover: handini_atmodiwiryo/Shutterstock; Chapter opener: Ilya Bolotov/Shutterstock; p.10: joyt/fotolia; p.13: Jeffrey Lermer; p.16: Perfect Gui/Shutterstock; p.21: Monkey Business/fotolia; p.24: Rtimages/fotolia; p.33: Cineberg/iStock; p.40: davidmariuz/iStock; p.48: Cigdem/fotolia; p.56: NicoElNino/iStock; p.64: guvendemir/iStock; p.72: mizar_21984/fotolia; p.77: monkeybusinessimages/iStock; p.80: Hoda Bogdan/fotolia; p.92: TuTheLens/iStock; p.98: LuckyBusiness/iStock; p.104: AdamGregor/iStock; p.109: Alexander Raths/fotolia; p.114: Baloncici/Shutterstock; p.117: fotokris/iStock; p.122: photoeverywhere/fotolia; p.128: GreenApple78/iStock; p.136: auremar/fotolia; p.140: vm/iStock; p.148: Tommy/fotolia; p.151: herreneck/fotolia; p.156: kupicoo/iStock; p.163: Cineberg/iStock; p.170: IK75/iStock; p.186: Jeffrey Lermer; p.188: Karen Wyrwas; p.189: Laurence Cobb

Every effort has been made to trace copyright holders for the works reproduced in this book, and the publisher apologises for any inadvertent omissions.

ISBN: 978-0-9956838-0-8

Contents

1. An introduction 9
2. What is so special about the construction industry? 15
3. Choosing the right trading structure for your construction business 23
4. Subcontractor or employee? 39
5. Bookkeeping 47
6. Making Tax Digital 55
7. The importance of performance monitoring 63
8. Cash flow issues 71
9. Outline of the Construction Industry Scheme 79
10. The future of the Construction Industry Scheme 97
11. Extracting remuneration 103
12. Assets 113
13. Ring-fencing 121
14. Pensions 127
15. Partnership and shareholder disputes 139

16	Contractor disputes	147
17	Guest chapter: Contracts	155
18	Guest chapter: Insurance	169
	Glossary	179
	About the authors	185

An introduction

1
An introduction

> "A successful man is one who can lay a firm foundation with the bricks that others throw at him."
> — *David Brinkley*

This is our second foray into the world of writing a book, and yet again we are faced with apprehension at the thought of the challenge that lies ahead. Despite this sense of trepidation, we are determined that this book will prove a useful tool, and feel genuinely privileged to have such a readily available and accessible platform through which we can share some of our broad experiences, in the hope of helping those people and businesses who operate in one of the most challenging environments in UK industry – namely, the construction sector.

The construction industry is a highly diversified sector which covers many aspects that are incredibly important to the UK economy; one might even argue that it is one of the foundations on which so much of the success of the economy is built. From the humblest self-employed tradesman to the largest commercial property developer, the construction industry drives and generates a huge amount of economic benefit, both directly and indirectly. Many ancillary businesses derive their trade through supplying this vast sector.

The industry faces unique pressures, scrutiny and increasing regulation from the authorities, much more so than many other sectors, and this challenging backdrop can prove incredibly difficult for construction businesses to negotiate, let alone be successful in. But, as the opening quote to this introduction said, success can sometimes be achieved by laying a firm foundation with whatever is thrown at you, and therein lies one of the primary aims of this book: how to lay and construct the 'bricks' that are thrown at you. Thereby creating a solid foundation for your business both to grow and prove resilient enough to withstand the pressures of an ever changing and challenging business landscape.

Who is this book aimed at?

If you work in the construction industry, then this book will undoubtedly contain useful information, regardless of whether you operate as a sole trader or run a larger, more established limited entity. The content will be useful for businesses such as:

- Scaffolders
- Self-employed subcontractors or tradesmen
- Builders
- Installation contractors
- Main contractors
- Professionals who operate in the industry – such as architects and surveyors
- Brick workers

The book is not specifically aimed at residential or commercial property developers, although if you do operate as one then you may find some of the content useful, especially in respect of your engagements with subcontractors.

Why should I read this book?

There is no magic formula to achieving success in the construction sector, or any sector for that matter. A business is not like a handily numbered construction set, with all the pieces slotting together to form one wonderfully oiled precision piece of equipment – invariably there is always an annoying piece that seems to be missing...

In this book we will examine and learn to understand the unique pressures facing many construction businesses, and look at solutions to help businesses not just survive, but **thrive!** Over the course of the following chapters, we will take a systematic look at how best to structure, manage, operate and optimise your business, as well as offering innovative proposals that could help make your company more agile and less susceptible to any potential pitfalls offered up by the existing (and future) regulatory framework of this vitally important sector. In examining these needs, and how they affect your business, we aim to give you an insight into the industry within which your company operates, and to provide some knowledge that will help you make important decisions and the right choices.

As mentioned earlier, the construction sector is highly specialised, with many unique features and inherent complexities. It is probably true to say that most accountants lack **real** expertise in this sector and, whilst you can get away with a lack of in-depth expertise in more straightforward sectors, the challenges of the Construction Industry Scheme can mean that any compromise in your choice of accountant could result in poor advice and bad decisions.

We have acted in this sector for many years now and have been fortunate to work with some exceptional people. We have experienced many of the changes that have helped shape the construction industry, including sitting on the Association of Certified Chartered Accountants (ACCA) Global Forum for Taxation which advised throughout the latest rewrite of the Construction Industry Scheme rules, so we feel well placed to be able to offer our expertise in this sector.

We believe an accountant is more than an office that you interact with once or twice year to meet filing obligations or to seek help with an issue; it is more of a partnership, with both parties working together and sharing their expertise in pursuit of a common goal – namely, success.

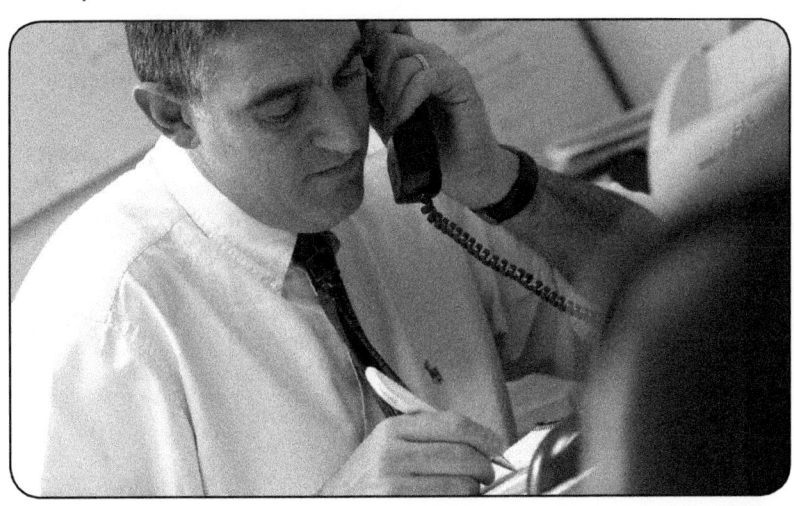

What is so special about the construction industry?

> "The nail that sticks out the furthest, gets hammered the hardest."
>
> — *Anon*

The construction industry is a key driver of the UK economy, generating over £100 billion in annual economic output, and employing over 2.1 million staff – which represents almost 6.5% of the total UK workforce*. Growth, which stagnated during the post-recessionary period, has returned with a vengeance, partly driven by government spending on infrastructure projects and targeted policy direction, whilst the private sector – which accounts for almost 75% of total annual construction revenue – is benefiting from improvements in consumer demand and the overall economy.

Despite its apparent importance to the UK economy, the construction industry is a somewhat special beast, with many unique characteristics that set it apart from most other industry sectors. The most important of these characteristics are as follows:

- The industry is generally not trusted by HM Revenue & Customs (HMRC)
- It suffers from low margins
- It is subject to more special rules and regulations than other business sectors
- It operates against the backdrop of a harsh penalty regime
- Businesses operate in an environment of special payment methods which can exacerbate cash flow pressures

The attitude of HMRC

The first, and perhaps most major difference, is the attitude of HMRC towards the sector; in fact, as the opening quote said: the nail that sticks out the furthest, gets hammered the most,

*http://www.parliament.uk/briefing-papers/sn01432.pdf (2014)

and judging by the perception of many businesses we speak to, HMRC has no qualms when it comes to whacking you on the thumb!

HMRC has traditionally been mistrustful of the industry, viewing it as a non-compliant sector which has consistently been the cause of much loss of tax revenues for the Exchequer. More so than other industries, it is subject to intense scrutiny and a changing compliance, reporting and regulatory framework, as evidenced by the almost perpetual introduction of new Construction Industry Schemes (CIS). This attitude obviously provides a challenging backdrop for businesses to operate in, many of whom are already struggling with the day-to-day demands of running successful businesses in the twenty-first century. The heavy-handed approach has resulted in an environment which places a great administrative burden on businesses; a burden that is further exacerbated by a progressively harsh penalty regime which can be triggered by the most minor of infractions. It is arguable whether this climate is conducive to establishing mutual respect and co-operation between businesses and HMRC and, unfortunately, as we will see in later chapters, the future attitude of the authorities is unlikely to shift dramatically if recent HMRC consultation documents are anything to go by.

Differing payment methods and the effect on cash flow

The framework imposed by HMRC has led to a unique set of payment methods, with some businesses often having to suffer a withholding tax in the form of CIS deductions. Those businesses fortunate enough to be entitled to payment without deduction (known as gross payment status) often have to operate with the constant threat of having this payment status revoked by HMRC for certain compliance failures. Obviously, cash flow is critical across all industries, but especially so in the construction industry where inherently low margins and a widespread CIS deduction policy make it even more important to have effective cash flow management in place. Sometimes larger jobs in the sector are completed on an application for payment basis, with regular staged payments from customers being released once the actual work to date has been valued by a surveyor or similar professional. This opens up further issues and potential cash flow problems, especially if works have been held up, delayed or not completed to specified requirements.

Furthermore, throughout the lifetime of a contract, there may be variations, snagging or the need to make good unsatisfactory work; all of which adds a great deal of cost uncertainty. Even when payment has been made, additional cash deductions such as retentions can also be imposed as a method of hedging against any defects that need to be righted following completion of a contract, or against other contractual contingencies; releasing this retention, which might be 2–5% of the overall contract value, can often require a significant amount of time.

Of course, despite all these potential revenue deductions and problems, companies must continue to buy materials, operate plant and machinery, and fund the workforce (with subcontractors quite often paid weekly for regular piece work) – failure to do so means that jobs cannot progress satisfactorily and customer payments are not so forthcoming. These factors all make the construction industry a special sector in which to operate, and by special we do not mean privileged.

Other issues

Whilst HMRC does its best impression of a blunt instrument, the natural complexity of the regulatory framework together with small margins, pressures on cash flow and a traditionally adversarial relationship between contractors and subcontractors, means that the industry is particularly prone to dispute. Even in the best of cases, disputes can prove costly both financially and from a reputational perspective, whilst worst-case scenarios often don't bear thinking about.

Thankfully, there is a robust dispute resolution system in the UK, but the overall impression remains: **this is a highly challenging environment in which to operate, and one that compares unfavourably to other industries**. It is, therefore, essential to take effective measures to protect yourself and your business, and a good starting point might include taking note of the following:

- Negotiating and maintaining good terms with suppliers
- Maintaining a good compliance record with HMRC
- Dealing quickly with any potential contractual disputes
- Effectively managing cash flow
- Monitoring costs and reacting swiftly to key performance indicators and other management information
- Ensuring quality standards are met on all jobs
- Effectively managing project and cost accounting to ensure tenders are not priced too low

It's not all doom and gloom; whilst we've skirted over how HMRC views the industry and how it generally implements unhelpful and unwieldly regulation, having a thorough understanding of HMRC and the CIS will help your business to establish a robust structure, both legally and operationally, to be able to cope with the numerous demands of working in the modern construction sector. This book aims to help you to achieve that goal.

Construction Industry Training Board (CITB) levy

Despite its name, the CITB levy is just another tax that the construction sector is faced with. The CITB levy is, purportedly, a contribution that CITB-registered employers in the construction industry make to support the skills and training of employees in the sector, and fund growth for businesses. The reality is that this is seldom the case, with monies collected not going into an earmarked pool reserved for the industry.

The level of contribution is based upon the total annual wage bill, including both Pay As You Earn (PAYE) employees and CIS subcontractors. For 2016, registered employers with an annual wage bill under £80,000 per year do not have to pay (but still need to complete the annual levy return). Businesses whose total wage bill exceeds £80,000 must pay a levy of 0.5% of total PAYE due for the year, plus 1.25% of the total net CIS subcontractor payments. Those businesses with annual wages bills between £80,001 and £400,000 receive a 50% reduction in the levy. Filing an annual levy return is also required.

Choosing the right trading structure for your construction business

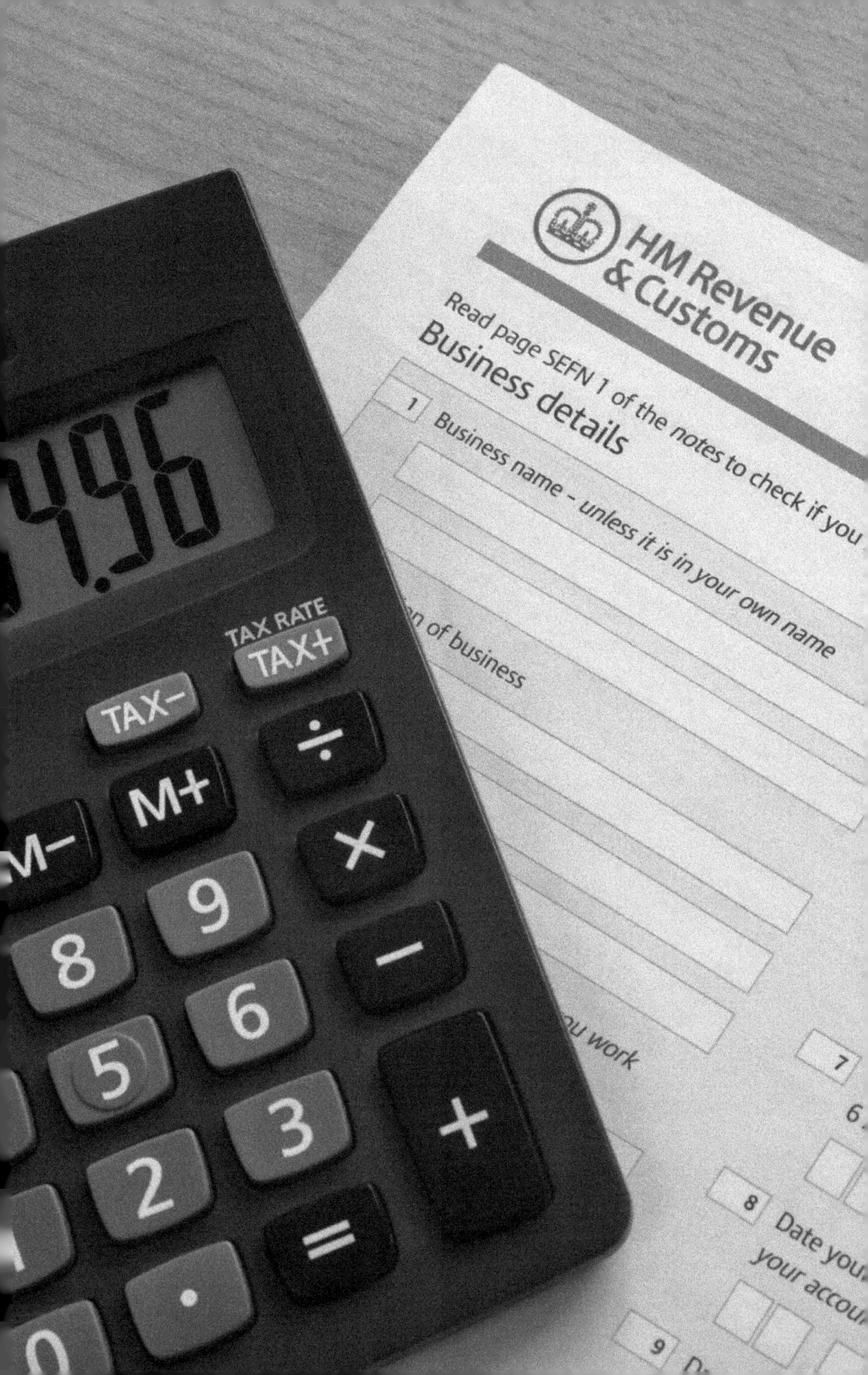

HM Revenue & Customs

Read page SEFN 1 of the notes to check if you

Business details

1 Business name – unless it is in your own name

~~n~~ of business

~~ou~~ work

7

6

8 Date you
your accou~~nt~~

9 D~~

> "If you really look closely, most overnight successes took a long time."
> — Steve Jobs

In the UK there are three main vehicles from which to operate a business:

- As a self-employed sole trader or partnership
- With a limited liability company
- With a limited liability partnership

With a limited liability partnership

Each of these structures has its own specific strengths and weaknesses which define its suitability for differing business activities. In addition to this, they also vary in the extent of statutory regulations that must be adhered to, and consequently there is a differential in the relative costs associated with setting up and maintaining these entities.

You will undoubtedly be running your construction business through one of these vehicles, and a brief goal of this chapter is to demonstrate the individual characteristics of each – both benefits and disadvantages – that will assist you in deciding whether this is the most optimal vehicle for your circumstances, and if any structural change – now or in future – is necessary.

Self-employed sole trader

Setting up as a sole trader is by far the simplest and potentially cheapest method of operating a business. As the title suggests, you are providing services in your own name, and dealing with your suppliers and customers directly. Being self-employed allows you to claim relief on legitimate business expenses incurred whilst carrying out your construction trade, by offsetting these costs against your income when you complete your annual self-assessment tax return.

The construction industry has many self-employed tradesmen, often working as subcontractors for other organisations. On the whole, trading as a sole trader is a relatively simple, cost effective method of operating.

Registering as self-employed

When you begin self-employment you must register with HMRC for tax purposes. You should do this as soon as possible after commencement since failing to register within three months of starting will result in a financial penalty, and the possibility of incurring further penalties for a prolonged failure to register. Thankfully, registering is fairly straightforward and can either be done online by visiting HMRC's website: www.online.hmrc.gov.uk/shortforms/form/CWF1ST or by telephoning HMRC's newly created self-employed helpline on 0300 200 3500.

Registering for CIS

Registering for CIS is a requirement for self-employed tradespeople who work in the construction sector. As with most governmental taxes, the application process is straightforward and can be done with a quick telephone call to HMRC's CIS Helpline on 0300 200 3210. You will need to provide both your National Insurance number and 10-digit unique tax reference number.

Registering for Value Added Tax (VAT)

Voluntarily registering for VAT could be beneficial for a sole trader if you are providing services to exclusively VAT registered businesses. It will add a veneer of professionalism which can have a positive effect on the perception other businesses may have of you, as well as providing a slight cost advantage in allowing you to reclaim VAT on some of your business expenses. Charging VAT on your services will also give you a short-term cash flow advantage as you will be receiving an additional 20% on any income generated. Of course, you are legally holding this money on behalf of HMRC for a short period before you need to pay it following submission of your quarterly VAT returns.

Unfortunately, VAT isn't an optional tax – as soon as your business turnover exceeds a certain threshold (currently £83,000 per annum) you have a legal obligation to register and to begin accounting for it. The penalties in place for failing to do so can be quite severe, so consult your accountant if you exceed or are likely to approach this threshold within the next 12-month period.

Operating a business bank account

One common pitfall of sole traders is a failure to open a dedicated business bank account, with many continuing to use their own personal bank accounts. Having a dedicated business account increases the transparency between your personal and business affairs, and in the event of any HMRC enquiry into your finances you will easily be able to prove and differentiate between business income and expenditure, and any personal income or expenditure. Unfortunately, the construction sector is fairly prone to compliance checks from HMRC, so ensuring you have a separate business bank account is important for protecting your status in the eyes of the authorities, even if any compliance check is not aimed at you, but at a contractor who is engaging you.

Most high street banks offer periods of free banking, and are particularly keen to attract new business customers. Some even offer free banking for life, so take some time to explore all the various options available to you.

Keeping good records of your transactions

Having a business bank account is a perfect way to record your business activities, and can be a useful tool in differentiating your business expenditure from personal expenses. There is a legal requirement for businesses to keep records for six years following the end of the tax year that the records relate to. In this case, the definition of records includes the aforementioned bank account information, as well as any invoices or receipts for items you have purchased, and details of any remittances or invoices for services that you have provided.

Professional insurance

Check with an accredited insurance broker to ensure you have suitable business insurance for your trade. See Chapter 18 'Insurance' for more information.

The self-employed test – protecting yourself

In certain circumstances, HMRC may dispute a qualification to operate as self-employed. Following on from this, how the HMRC views you will impact on how you are treated for tax and National Insurance purposes. This issue is especially important in the construction industry, with its history of compliance problems and an overzealous approach by HMRC. Chapter 4 'Subcontractor or employee?' goes into this employment status in more detail.

The benefits of being a self-employed sole trader

Most of the benefits associated with being a sole trader revolve around the comparative simplicity of the format:

- Requires simpler year end accounts, which reduces administrative burden
- Less statutory paperwork
- Deferred tax payments
- Relatively inexpensive to operate
- Takes minimal effort to change the format to another trading style, i.e. to a limited company

- Offers confidentiality to owners with no statutory requirement to submit financial information nor ownership records into the public domain
- Straightforward method of withdrawing money from the business, with tax paid on profit not on what is withdrawn
- Potential for lower accountancy fees

The drawbacks of being self-employed

The major drawback in sole trading is that all of the services you provide, and all of the liabilities you accrue are carried out in your own name. In the event of any problems, it is you who is liable – whether you are unable to pay a supplier; enter into a messy dispute with a contractor; are unable to pay HMRC; or if a member of staff takes you to an employment tribunal – you have no protection. The ultimate responsibility for all liabilities associated with this business model is generally what makes this trading style unattractive in most circumstances.

Remember your personal assets, including your home, are potentially at risk. In today's litigious climate, we usually discourage this method of trading, especially given some of the inherent risks associated with the construction industry.

CASE STUDY – The risks of self-employment

We had a client who traded in a partnership who was facing bankruptcy because his main contractor, a developer with whom he had worked for many years, went bust. Fortunately, we managed to save him by doing a partnership voluntary arrangement which meant that he kept his house, although he did face seven years of costs. **The moral of this is that, despite your best efforts, if you trade in a self-employed manner, then 'unlimited liability' will place you at considerable risk from factors outside your control.**

The limited liability company

A limited liability company is an independent business structure and is one of the most popular vehicles from which to operate a business. This popularity partly stems from the fact that the owners of the company, the shareholders, enjoy a degree of protection from any liabilities that the company may acquire. Their liability is limited to the amount that the shareholders invest into the business, so long as they act reasonably and honestly in complying with company law.

A brief overview of company formation

In the UK all company formations are handled through Companies House, although many new businesses often make use of a third party, such as an accountant or a company formation agent, to carry out the actual incorporation. The costs are fairly reasonable, and the information required is straightforward:

- Names of directors
- Number of shares
- Names of the shareholders
- The benefit and rights the shares hold
- The registered office

The final element in forming a new company is to prepare the Memorandum and Articles of Association (M&A). This document represents the constitution of the company, and as such records and governs some of the internal mechanisms of the company.

Shortly after being formed at Companies House, new companies will receive notification from HMRC. This notification comes as a form CT41G. This form will provide a Unique Tax Reference (UTR) for the company, as well as asking for some further information on the company to ensure HMRC's records are up to date, primarily so they do not miss the opportunity to start collecting taxes. Who said government was inefficient?

Separate legal personality

Despite being owned by its shareholders, the company has a distinct separate legal personality. It has its own bank account and pays its own tax based on the profit that it makes and – unlike a sole trader – the owner's personal tax liabilities bear no relation to the profit made by the company.

Because the company is a separate legal entity, the directors and officers of the company have certain duties and responsibilities:

- **Fiduciary Duties** – to act in good faith for the best interests of the company, not to make secret profits, act for proper purposes and avoid conflict of interests
- **Common Law Duties** – carry out duties with reasonable skill and care
- **Statutory Duties** – duty to creditors and employees, and adherence to the latest iteration of the Companies Act

Breaching these duties and obligations can lead to disqualification from acting as a director, and, in extreme circumstances, criminal proceedings.

It is also important to realise that the company's money is not the owners' money; consequently, when the directors or shareholders withdraw money from the company there may exist certain tax implications of doing so.

The benefits of operating a limited liability company

As the name suggests, the principal benefit of trading as a limited company is the limited liability of the company's shareholders and officers. As long as the company is operated legally and within the terms of the Companies Act, the personal assets of the officer and shareholders are not at risk in the event of any business failure or winding up. In the event of any insolvency, the assets of the company – insofar as they may exist – are used to pay any debts; the shareholders are only liable to the extent of the value of their unpaid shares, and the officers are free to incorporate another company.

Operating a limited company often gives suppliers and customers a sense of confidence. We saw how perception was a factor in operating as a sole trader; it also plays a part for a limited company, but with a more positive effect. In fact, many larger contractors or businesses in particular will prefer not to deal with non-limited businesses.

Potentially, running a limited company **may** result in you paying a lower rate of tax and, with the rate of corporation tax scheduled to fall during coming years, any benefits of paying a lower tax rate is likely to be enhanced in future, although the introduction of additional tax on dividends from April 2016 reduces the benefit slightly, but not altogether.

The drawbacks of operating a limited liability company

The most important point, and one that is commonly misunderstood even by those who own a company, is that the profits (and assets) of the company are the property of the company, and do not belong to the shareholders (owners) or officers. In fact, if company property is unlawfully diverted to the shareholders they may be prosecuted for theft, not to mention any unpleasant tax consequences. The benefits of limited liability do not come without a price.

The other consideration in operating a limited company is the greater administrative and compliance burden that it places on the officers over being self-employed. There is a wide range of information that must be handled, recorded and published, and deadlines to be met – all packaged up in an escalating regime of penalties for failing to comply. Of course, if you use a good accountant, then meeting your compliance obligations should be seamless and the risk of penalties mitigated.

The limited liability partnership (LLP)

The LLP is a relatively recent innovation in the business world, and was the latest business vehicle to be introduced, receiving official Royal Assent in 2000. It can be loosely described as a hybrid between a limited liability company and a traditional self-employment partnership, in that it offers the limited liability available to owners of limited companies combined with the tax regime and flexibility available to partnerships.

LLPs were originally designed, and indeed partly instigated, by professional partnerships such as accountants, lawyers and architects. They felt the need to limit their own personal liability that may have arisen out of any mistakes created by another partner.

However, many other types of businesses can benefit from operating out of a LLP.

Brief overview of LLP formation

In much the same way as limited companies, an LLP is incorporated through Companies House. Unlike companies which have officers (directors) and owners (shareholders), the LLP is run and owned by its 'partners', who are referred to as members. The members of the LLP usually make an agreement between themselves as to their respective rights and profit entitlements, or on how to treat retiring members or appoint new members, and there is a great deal of flexibility in the ability to separate out different rights. This mirrors some of the constitutional aspects of a limited company, such as the class and benefits of different shares, or the covenants contained within the Articles of Association. The partnership agreement is important, especially in the construction sector which is notorious for the frequency of its disputes.

Laying down these ground rules in a formal partnership agreement is important as LLPs do not have a legal requirement to create a formal agreement between its members upon creation.

Running an LLP

Many of the caveats we covered in respect of the previous vehicles hold true for LLPs. So, be advised that you must:

- Maintain adequate accounting records
- Be aware that the LLP has a separate legal personality, continuing to exist independently of its members
- Prepare and submit information to Companies House for publication across the public domain
- Submit information regarding the members' individual profit shares to the public domain once certain thresholds have been exceeded
- Submit partnership tax returns to HMRC
- Ensure suitable insurance is in place, both for individual members and the LLP as a separate entity

The benefits of operating an LLP

Members enjoy:
- No employer's National Insurance. Members' income is not subject to this 13.8% tax
- Significant delay in paying their personal tax as opposed to PAYE

- Generous (or, as some might argue, fair and sensible) car and motor benefits
- No tax liability for using LLP assets for personal use.
- No tax liability on introducing new members – unlike limited companies where there may exist a tax liability in giving away shares in the company.
- Potential loss relief benefits, allowing members to immediately offset losses against other income, either in the same year or previous years. Limited companies must record a profit before being allowed to offset losses.
- Paying taxes just on their share of the overall LLP profit, similar to a sole trader, and suffer no tax on remuneration drawings. HMRC has clamped down on so-called 'salaried members', with changes to the employment status of certain members of LLPs, which would bring them into the PAYE/NI regime and outside of self-employment.

The members also enjoy some degree of protection from the liabilities of the LLP, so long as they do not act fraudulently or trade wrongfully. This level of liability is limited to the amount they have invested; they cannot lose more than this.

Disadvantages of an LLP

As the name suggests, an LLP is a partnership. Therefore it needs at least two partners. This raises issues of trust; if one partner falls out with the other and leaves then the LLP is dissolved unless another partner can be introduced. This is easily overcome with sleeping partners or corporate partners, but it could still be considered as a potential drawback, therefore ensuring a comprehensive partnership agreement is in place is vital.

The legal requirements to prepare and publish annual accounts add to the administrative burden. Additionally, certain profit distributions to members in high grossing LLPs will need to be disclosed on the public record, removing a certain element of privacy and confidentiality. These legal requirements also extend to the members who must, like limited company officers, behave and act within the confines of the law. Failure can result in prosecution and future disqualification from being a member or director in another business.

Even though the LLP has its own separate legal identity, dealings with third parties, for example banks, may still require the members to provide their own personal guarantees, much in the same manner as these guarantees apply to directors of limited companies.

Recommended structure

The actual structure that is best suited to your business will depend on your circumstances and the plans you have for your company, both currently and for the future. From a professional perspective, we have virtually no sole trader or unincorporated partnerships operating in the construction sector because of the risks of personal liability.

Vehicle	Characteristics	Advantages	Disadvantages
Sole Trader	Not a separate legal entity Owner pays tax on net profit No tax due on drawings	Confidentiality: no accounts published into public domain Tax paid on profit, not drawings Inexpensive to operate Simple accounts	Perception problem Certain trades may be vulnerable to employment status check No protection from liability Potential for higher rate tax CIS tax suffered can only be reclaimed via annual personal tax return, leading to potential cash flow disadvantage
Limited Company	Separate legal entity Pays corporation tax on profits Potential tax on remuneration Prepares accounts for Companies House	More professional perception as business Owners protected from liabilities Low corporation tax rate CIS tax suffered can be offset against PAYE/NI tax payable to HMRC	Accounts in the public domain Administrative costs and burden Assets belong to company not the owners Directors have legal obligations
Limited Liability Partnership	Separate legal entity Members pay personal tax on their share of profit No tax due on members drawings LLP pays no tax itself Prepares accounts for Companies House	Members protected from liabilities Flexible structure No tax on change of structure or succession Tax benefits for members	Accounts in the public domain and more detailed Administrative costs and burden Requires at least two partners and a degree of trust or partnership agreement Potential for higher rate tax CIS tax suffered is treated in the same manner as for sole traders leading to potential cash flow disadvantage

Jeffrey Lermer and Karen Wyrwas — Breaking Ground

Subcontractor or employee?

> "Action is the key to success."
>
> — *Picasso*

We saw in the previous chapter how fixated HMRC is on the employment status of workers. Throughout the past forty years, the various evolutions of construction industry schemes have had this issue at their heart with increasing compliance checks and the implementation of stricter penalty regimes, all designed to crack down on the loss of tax revenue that can arise when workers are incorrectly classified as self-employed rather than as employees.

Ensuring that workers are correctly classified remains one of the most contentious issues facing businesses that operate in the construction industry. As a contractor you are solely responsible for the correct classification of your workers and, under the CIS, you must make a statutory declaration each month confirming that you have verified the employment status of your workers. Any failure to correctly classify and therefore account for the right amount of tax is virtually guaranteed to lead to extensive financial penalties. Furthermore, HMRC has adopted a fervent, almost zealous approach to employment status and successfully challenging its assertions in relation to status is an activity that requires a keen understanding of the complexities involved.

Bearing this in mind, this chapter will attempt to navigate a course through the whole employed versus self-employed minefield, paying particular focus on the approach by HMRC – from legislative definitions and compliance, through to disputes and the penalty regimes. Understanding the approach of the authorities will help you to devise and implement robust employment status procedures which may limit any potential risks in this area.

The problem

The UK has an overregulated labour market, with employees generally being entitled to a great deal of benefits and employment rights from day one. Whilst this is good for employees, there is a clear economic impact on employers, with National Insurance, pensions and holiday pay, for example, all increasing the payroll cost of full-time employees. This makes the use of self-employed workers an attractive option, and whilst this practice is not unique to the construction sector, the somewhat flexible and temporal nature of construction contracts naturally lends itself to the use of flexible, self-employed workers.

Why self-employed?

The common misconception is that self-employed staff are cheaper than employed staff; of course there may be some economic benefit, such as no employers' National Insurance, holiday pay, sick or maternity pay and redundancy, but the primary benefits lie in flexibility, i.e. only having to pay for labour when required, and less ownership and responsibility of the employer over the rights of the worker.

The status of workers

The employment status of workers is not a matter of choice, nor is it defined by whether a worker has registered with HMRC as a self-employed subcontractor. Moreover, it is a matter of fact. There are three status tests which HMRC often use as a guide for identifying whether a worker is acting in a self-employed fashion (providing a **contract for services**) or whether they are to be treated as employees (operating under a **contract of service**). They are:

- Control
- Personal service
- Basis of payment

The **control** test is usually considered indicative of employment when there exists a level of interference in **how** a job should be done and by whom. Self-employed workers generally receive less interference from a contractor and can exert more control over how, where and when a specific job may be carried out. However, the control test is open to differing views on interpretation, so care must be taken if you are relying on this status test as the sole method for establishing the employment status of workers. In particular, contractors should be prepared to defend any accusation or evidence of:

- Interfering in how a job is done
- Requiring workers to be available
- Specifying what tasks are performed, and in what order

The obligation for a worker to provide a **personal service** is another fact that is usually indicative of employment rather than self-employment; essentially this means that the worker is providing the services of just himself, as is normally the case in paid employment. HMRC, following some high-profile legal challenges, now acknowledges that where a worker has the right to provide a **substitute worker** then this work cannot be under contract of service, i.e. cannot be classed as employment.

HMRC often cite the **basis for payment** as being a key factor in determining the employment status of workers, and a major assumption is that self-employed workers are often paid a set price for a 'job' and must absorb any additional costs themselves should this job take longer or involve more work than was initially quoted. By contrast, employees are typically paid a salary, or on a pro rata basis – for example per hour, week or month. Despite this distinction, there still remains some contention since it is not uncommon for certain self-employed construction workers to be paid by the hour or day. In general, the basis for payment test is held in a better light if factors such as the potential for financial loss or risk – which an employee would never have – are considered as well.

An important note regarding employment status: certain workers, for example labourers (who are paid by the hour), foremen or supervisors, and heavy plant operators are generally classified as 'employees' – **but** this classification is highly situational and not set in stone, so, as with most issues in this area, be wary and be prepared.

The following bullet points provide a brief summary of the most common employment status indicators:

Employed
- The contractor has the right to control what the worker does, where, when and how – even if this right is not exercised
- Worker only supplies small tools
- Worker does not risk his or her money, and there is no possibility of financial loss
- Worker has no business organisation, i.e. no yard, office, vehicles, staff or bank account
- Worker is paid by the hour, day, week or month

Self-employed
- Worker has the right to decide how and when the work is done within an overall deadline
- Worker supplies materials, plant and heavy equipment
- Worker 'bids' for a job and must absorb any additional costs
- Worker has the right to hire additional workers who are paid by him
- Worker paid a fixed rate for the job regardless of actual time taken or costs to himself incurred

Whilst this summary is by no means exhaustive, it should prove a useful checklist to ensure that your business is protected in the event of any future compliance review.

HMRC enforcement

We mentioned how the issue of employment status was a major bugbear for HMRC, and how the various iterations of construction industry schemes have been developed to try to crack down on the perceived misclassification of workers and to allay potential losses in tax revenues. HMRC have kindly adopted a mantra of 'helping construction businesses get their employment status right' – whilst at the same time adopting a rather unhelpful attitude of generally mistrusting construction businesses and a readiness to invoke an extremely harsh penalty regime. There are no kid gloves where HMRC is involved – the best defence is a good defence!

HMRC has committed significant resources to policing employment status – more status inspectors, extra compliance and CIS teams, as well as extensive investment in online resources that can allow rapid cross-checking of businesses and red flag potential compliance risks; all as part of a wide-ranging ambition to reclaim what it regards as loss of taxes as a result of worker status. As well as this, they also receive tip-offs from disgruntled suppliers, customers or ex-employees; have access to CIS and CITB returns; and can make enquiries through examining individual subcontractor self-assessment tax returns. The odds are clearly stacked in their favour, and, as technology and reporting requirements increase in complexity and regularity, HMRC will benefit from greater levels of scrutiny across the construction industry.

Against this backdrop, it is important to understand and manage the status of workers, both for now and for the future. If you are unlucky enough to fall foul of an Employer Compliance Review, then the first thing you should do is to have a quick look over any invoices you have from self-employed subcontractors. HMRC, in particular, will generally review these invoices as a first step of any compliance review, and typically look for the invoice to have some or all of the following characteristics:

- Show the worker's home address
- Have an amateurish look, with consecutive numbering
- Contain narrative that indicates 'labour only'
- The shown bank account is a personal bank account
- The frequency of the invoices being issued: are they weekly, which could be problematic, or are they for a complete job?

Of course, invoices in this format are not indicative of employment or self-employment; however, if the invoices from your subcontractors are similar to this, then you should expect HMRC to investigate further. Similarly, HMRC will investigate any payments to individuals that have no supporting invoice.

What happens if I get it wrong?

It is important to get the employment status right as you are required to make a declaration each month. This means that you will be vulnerable to any subsequent compliance check, with a potential risk for penalties which could reach £3,000 per month, not to mention having to be liable for unpaid taxes or National Insurance. **Therefore, ignore this at your peril.**

HMRC does provide an online Employment Status Indicator (ESI) that contractors can use to reassure themselves on the status of their workers. It is anonymous, but the resulting report can be printed and retained on file as a method of defence against any future HMRC query into the employment status of the worker(s) in question.

Jeffrey Lermer and Karen Wyrwas — Breaking Ground

5 Bookkeeping

> "Many of life's failures are people who did not realize how close they were to success when they gave up."
>
> — *Thomas Edison*

If cash flow is the lifeblood of a business, then bookkeeping is quite possibly the thing that keeps all the blood flowing. Its importance to your business cannot be overstated, yet it is often under appreciated and low on the list of expenditure priorities.

Effective bookkeeping is about getting the basics right. If you can't manage the basics, then hope for the rest of the business is somewhat forlorn. The basics of a good bookkeeping system, for any business, should encompass the following:

- Recording all receipts or invoices from suppliers
- Recording all invoices issued to customers
- Recording transactions that are made through bank accounts, and reconciling them to bank statements
- Recording and reconciling petty cash transactions
- Allocating payments from customers
- Allocating payments to suppliers, and reconciling invoices and payments to supplier statements
- Maintaining the general ledger using the double entry system
- Maintaining a register of fixed assets, including allocating depreciation
- Recording and reconciling transactions for VAT purposes
- Recording accruals and prepayments on a predetermined basis
- Filing and maintaining the prime records, cross referencing to transactions entered into the bookkeeping system
- Preparing relevant reports for use by the company, including credit control reports, details of outstanding supplier accounts, monthly trial balances, profit and loss, balance sheets, VAT reports and bank reconciliations

It is important that the tasks listed on the previous page are carried out by someone who is familiar with the fundamental principles of bookkeeping and the construction industry.

These basics form the foundation of your internal accounting and finance functions and, as such, care must be taken that all information is recorded accurately and in a timely manner for it to be most worthwhile. To help with this, bookkeeping is best maintained when broken down into periods, such as months: each month is processed, checked, reconciled, then closed down once everything is agreed and the relevant reports have been printed or filed. The process continues for subsequent periods.

It is important to get these basics right, and to be thorough and disciplined; making important decisions based on inaccurate assumptions and information could have serious consequences. Furthermore, you may be required to provide some or even all of this information in the event of any HMRC investigation and the more documentary evidence you provide, generally the better the outcome is for you.

Why is it so important?

Bookkeeping is important as the first step of your accounting process, and without it you will struggle to extract, analyse and act upon information that is vital to your business. Other key benefits include:

- Provides vital information that helps you make important decisions regarding the financial management of your business
- Forms the basis of management information
- Helps with credit control, providing access to up-to-date information about monies that are outstanding
- Protects you in the event of any investigation by HMRC, by acting as an accurate record of all the financial transactions of your business

- Bookkeeping packages often assist with HMRC reporting obligations, providing easy to use functionality for submitting VAT returns or CIS300 returns
- Helps with compliance, by encouraging an environment of record-keeping and organisation
- Offers control and transparency over finances
- May help with tender or bidding processes by offering accurate financial and costing information
- May reduce annual accountancy or audit fees with well-maintained records requiring less work for accountants to process and report
- In larger organisations, it can relieve some of the administrative burden from other financial staff, allowing them to spend more time preparing more detailed analysis and reports

This list is by no means exhaustive, but you can clearly see the benefits.

Project accounting

As a contractor you need to know at any given moment the exact financial position your company has in any given project, and need a reliable project accounting process to record and access information. If you have good bookkeeping processes to manage the flow of this information, then you can easily determine your financial position in any project at any time. When projects tie up your capital it prevents you from investing or starting other projects. In this sector timing is essential to making profit. If you don't have the capital available to commence the next job or allocate elsewhere, then you may have some downtime in the future.

What form of bookkeeping suits you?

Bookkeeping comes in different forms and may require different levels of resources to be effective and useful; individual circumstances will dictate which aligns best with your needs. You may find you need a full-time internal bookkeeper as part of your finance team; or, if your business is smaller or has fewer transactions, then a less formal part-time arrangement may be adequate. Larger organisations will often have numerous bookkeeping personnel, with each taking responsibility for different aspects – purchases, sales or bank transactions, for example.

Bookkeeping software packages

Much bookkeeping nowadays is performed using specialist software packages, or combinations of packages. These are extremely powerful and can speed up your record-keeping and, therefore, shorten the time it takes to perform certain tasks, such as extracting management information, preparing debtor reports or assisting credit control, lists of outstanding bills and bank reconciliations. As packages have become more powerful, bookkeepers have generally increased their knowledge base and skills, using the software almost as a surrogate teacher. Furthermore, the market leading software packages are so commonplace that finding a bookkeeper who isn't familiar with them is virtually unheard of.

The functionality of these packages has also evolved, with many of them integrating the most common HMRC reporting obligation within the software – essentially, one package can be a one-stop shop for bookkeeping and submission of VAT, Payroll and CIS returns to HMRC. The drive across software packages is towards cloud computing; this means data isn't stored locally, and can be accessed from anywhere with an internet connection, adding more flexibility to your bookkeeping if you have a bookkeeper who cannot make it to your premises, but can access data from home. It also allows you, the owner, to access financial management reports remotely too. So if you are negotiating offsite for a vehicle lease, for example, you would be able to instantly prove affordability by generating cash flow, profit and loss, or other information on the financial position of your business at the click of a button.

The choice of package will be a personal one, and no doubt influenced by the skillset of bookkeeping staff. Newer products, such as Kashflow or Xero, offer cheap, cloud-based bookkeeping functionality and are easy to use and flexible in their reporting capabilities; older legacy systems like Sage are more expensive but combine bookkeeping with some project-based accounting and reporting options. At the other end of the scale, there are specialist industry packages, such as Procore or Foundation, which provide powerful, holistic construction solutions that manage CIS, bookkeeping and project accounting. **Proper investment in an established software package will only enhance your bookkeeping capabilities, and therefore the derived benefits.**

Changes to reporting obligations for businesses – Making Tax Digital

The government set out its new **Making Tax Digital (MTD)** initiative in the March 2015 Budget and, following various consultations, announced in early 2017 the details of the biggest upheaval to the system of tax-related reporting since the introduction of self-assessment in 1996. This will prove to be a major area of concern to all businesses and so we have included some further details and discussion in the next chapter.

The MTD initiative will lead to business owners facing greater scrutiny and HMRC obligations, with the introduction of regular electronic data interchange (EDI) between businesses and the authorities heralding a new era of transparency and digital government. Driven by technology, this will result in business owners having to report to HMRC more regularly **from April 2018**.

- Sole traders reporting details of their businesses through a quarterly report, followed by an annual summary
- Businesses transitioning to quarterly reporting in respect of corporation tax affairs, in addition to existing VAT obligations
- Greater real time information reporting for employees, payroll, CIS and employer pensions

Although the final details have not been confirmed at the time of going to print, it is expected that individuals and businesses will only have thirty days from the end of a quarterly period in which to report their trading information to HMRC. Furthermore, we understand that the quarterly reports must be submitted via bookkeeping software, thereby **requiring** all businesses to utilise some sort of bookkeeping software. This will no longer be just a recommended option but an **essential** business tool.

Your accountant may be able to provide bookkeeping services or recommend someone suitable.

Making Tax Digital

From April 2018, the biggest ever upheaval in the way that taxpayers deal with HMRC will be phased in. Even though the legislation and final plans have not been released, we could not publish a book about accounting and tax without addressing this. This will affect you; **ignore it at your peril!**

What is Making Tax Digital?

The government's **Making Tax Digital (MTD)** initiative, which was announced in the March 2015 Budget, aims to increase transparency in the new digital age and will lead to business owners facing greater scrutiny and HMRC obligations. It is a bold move which is set to make HMRC one of the most digitally advanced tax administrations in the world. Taxpayers will benefit through being able to view a complete picture of their tax affairs at any time, in the form of their online **digital tax account** which pulls together information provided to HMRC from various sources, including employers, banks and other government departments. In this way, there should be no tax liability surprises at the end of the year.

Under MTD, taxpayers, companies and businesses will all be required to submit their accounts to HMRC on a **quarterly basis** and then submit a final, fifth set of accounts annually to make any year end adjustments. The quarterly reports will be due **within thirty days** of the end of the quarter, and these must be submitted electronically via the taxpayer's own bookkeeping software.

When accounts are submitted, will HMRC see a tidy, succinct, clear office: everything where it should be and a tax plan properly in place? Or will they see a mess, with corrections made after the year end which will provide them with the opportunity to ask questions? If businesses do not start to prepare and organise themselves for MTD, they will be playing directly into HMRC's hands. MTD will enable HMRC to easily detect and log any number of minor incongruities and justify raising an investigation into a taxpayer.

What needs to be done?

Although exact reporting requirements had not been released at the time of writing, it is expected that the quarterly report to HMRC will be a summary of the financial accounts and balance sheet, rather than details of every underlying transaction. The quarterly returns must be made within thirty days of the end of each quarter, and there will be a final (fifth) catch up return, which must be filed nine months after the year end, similar to the position now. For many, this will be a **fivefold** increase in reporting obligations!

As already noted, the accounts information must be submitted to HMRC **directly** from the taxpayer's bookkeeping system. So, all but a very small minority (those who genuinely cannot use digital tools due to religious reasons or for whom online filing is not reasonably practicable for reasons of disability, age, remoteness of location) will need to make use of a bookkeeping system capable of transferring this information over the internet.

Businesses will need to prepare themselves for this significant increase in reporting obligations. From our point of view, a positive outcome is that the government is now forcing businesses to use bookkeeping software, which we have been recommending as best practice for many years! We believe that **cloud-based** bookkeeping systems, in particular, will be vital for assisting businesses with their obligations under MTD. There has already been a massive increase in the use of cloud-based bookkeeping systems but MTD has ensured that they will now become an essential tool for businesses.

Those already used to submitting quarterly VAT returns will be one step ahead, although MTD will require significantly more information to be passed to HMRC. It is expected that particular attention will be given to financial outgoings from a business, especially payments which relate to an individual's income, such as dividends, which affect their personal tax liability.

A natural follow on from the increased reporting is expected to be earlier and more regular payments to HMRC. Nothing has been announced in this area, although the various consultation documents have mentioned that this could be a possible future development. Currently, HMRC are stating that this would be voluntary.

When will MTD start?

The government announced at the 2017 Spring Budget a one-year deferral from the mandating of Making Tax Digital for Business for unincorporated businesses and landlords with turnovers below the VAT threshold.

This means that only those businesses, self-employed people and landlords with turnovers greater than the VAT threshold will be required to start using the new digital service from April 2018.

Businesses, self-employed people and landlords will be required to start using the new digital service from:

- April 2018 if they have profits chargeable to Income Tax and pay Class 4 National Insurance Contributions (NICs) and their turnovers are greater than the VAT threshold
- April 2019 if they have profits chargeable to Income Tax and pay Class 4 NICs and their turnovers are below the VAT threshold
- April 2019 if they are registered for and pay VAT
- April 2020 if they pay Corporation Tax (CT).

The first quarterly reporting period will be three months after the start of the accounting period following the introduction. Therefore, a limited company with an accounting period from 1 June 2020 to 31 May 2021 will have to submit their first MTD quarterly return covering the period 1 June 2020 to 31 August 2020.

Who does MTD affect?

Under MTD, businesses will be divided into three categories, according to their turnover:

- Turnover of less than £10,000: these businesses will NOT be required to report quarterly.
- Turnover up to twice the VAT limit (so 2 × £83,000 = £166,000): these businesses will be able to report using a **cash basis** where reporting income and paying tax will be based on the cash generated and full tax relief given for all expenses, including capital items. This should make the accounts more intuitive, easier to understand and simpler to file.
- All other companies: it is expected that the quarterly reports will contain similar detailed information as currently being reported annually.

The implications of MTD

Accurate and considered bookkeeping records will be essential. In our experience, bookkeepers do not always seek to fully understand the transactions being recorded. In particular, it is critical that money being paid out of a company to the directors and shareholders is classified correctly. If incorrectly shown as income or dividends and reported to HMRC in this way, there could easily arise various misunderstandings as to the personal liabilities of the directors/shareholders, especially should the company subsequently go into liquidation when there is significant sensitivity with regards to funds paid out of a company.

Accountants will need to help their clients to put in place clear tax strategies which can be implemented throughout the year, rather than via adjustments made after the year end.

What are we planning to do about MTD?

We are currently reviewing all our clients' accounts and circumstances so that we can provide specific advice about the right way forwards for them. We anticipate providing our clients with various options and solutions:

- Offer training on using bookkeeping software and how to submit accounts electronically, ensuring that the client understands what content is required and how to fit this with their tax strategy.
- Produce a tailored tax strategy document explaining how remuneration and dividends are calculated, so these can be reported on a real time actual basis rather than as an annual adjustment which could be challenged by HMRC.
- We are expecting to take on the bookkeeping for a significant number of clients through our sister company, Modina. This will ensure that accurate records are filed and avoid misleading information being submitted to HMRC.
- Some clients will choose to submit information themselves without proper checking. We will aim to tidy up and make corrections in the final year end report, although clients will need to be aware that all adjustments will be carefully monitored by HMRC and could trigger potential HMRC enquiry problems.

Let MTD trigger an opportunity to enhance your financial control

We recently carried out some independent research into what businesses really want from their accountant, under the definition of 'proactive advice'. We found, almost unilaterally, our potential clients wanted help with:

- Hands on, up to date advice on their accounts
- What to do **now** based on the circumstances they are seeing now
- How to use key performance indicators to make their businesses better

With this in mind, we set up a system called **EXPERT EYE**. Under this system, regular monthly or quarterly management accounts are prepared, either by the client or us. We take an active role in reviewing the accounts and seeking out the strengths, opportunities, weaknesses and threats embodied within the numbers. We then discuss and work on these with the client to make their business stronger. This approach allows us to really get under the bonnet and help our clients achieve their goals, whatever they may be: growth, mitigating their tax liability or simply creating a great business!

Jeffrey Lermer and Karen Wyrwas

The importance of performance monitoring

7

The importance of performance monitoring

> "What you pay attention to, grows."
>
> — *Gardening proverb*

It may seem like an obvious statement to say that performance measurement is an integral part of business management. By identifying key company and project aims, owners are more likely to achieve success. But the only way of knowing whether those goals are being delivered is by identifying indicators of their success and using them to monitor the way the business is performing. These indicators are known as Key Performance Indicators, or KPIs.

Performance monitoring is especially important in the construction sector where margins are tight, cash flow is squeezed, and there exists a risk potential for contractual disputes in the event of delays, poor workmanship, defects or other 'measurable' problems.

To be a truly effective tool, KPIs need to be timely, relevant, targeted and consistent.

- **Timely** – the KPI needs to be measured so that results, in most cases, are available quickly to ensure that remedial action can be taken swiftly if necessary
- **Relevant** – measuring the right KPIs can help to improve the business, instead of attempting to derive a performance measure from something that exerts little importance on the business
- **Targeted & consistent** – results are best achieved when specifics are targeted, rather than broader measures, and where the measuring criteria remain consistent

They also need to lead to some actionable steps to achieve a goal; for example, creating a KPI to increase the number of new building projects you secure is unlikely to achieve its objective since there is no measurable component that results in a course of action.

When used correctly following these guidelines, KPIs can provide you with an immediate snapshot of the overall performance of your business. In an industry as competitive as the construction sector, it becomes vital for an owner to have real time data concerning the state of the business in conjunction with KPIs as a tool to gather vital decision-making information.

Identifying KPIs

Choosing the right indicators to monitor is dependent on those factors that you consider most important to your overall goals. For example, a business that supplies subcontracted labour would derive more benefit from measuring worker satisfaction levels than a site clearance contractor, whereas the site clearance contractor might wish to monitor waste or environmental indicators.

The key is identifying those indicators which are most representative and important to your success.

Benchmarking

Once you've identified the most relevant and important KPIs, you will need some form of benchmark to measure them against. Luckily, KPIs are very à la mode across the industry at the moment, and a great deal of information about common KPIs that are applicable to the construction sector is readily available. This presents an opportunity to select and compare your performance against similar businesses or the industry standard. This can provide almost instant gratification or disappointment but, regardless, will establish a realistic benchmark against which you can measure performance over a prolonged period of time, and which can be used to drive improvements.

Common KPIs in the construction sectors

A good starting point is to use some of the KPIs that are commonly used by construction businesses, as listed on the next page, taking into account the exact nature of the construction services you provide. Since these are commonly used, it should be relatively straightforward to acquire some industry standards as a starting benchmark. As time goes by you may develop new KPIs but remember to choose those that are most relevant and important; too much navel gazing can prove counterproductive or a distraction.

- Client satisfaction
- Defects
- Loss of materials or leakage
- Construction time and cost
- Productivity
- Profitability
- Health and safety
- Employee satisfaction
- Staff turnover
- Sickness absence
- Working hours
- Qualifications and skills
- Impact on environment
- Waste
- Commercial vehicle movements

Monitoring financial performance

The KPIs mentioned previously focused on measuring operational performance which is vital for helping you to improve and achieve your strategic goals. To get a comprehensive insight into your business it can also be useful to monitor financial performance. The result of this financial monitoring can assist with decision-making processes and help to identify potential risks to mitigate, or problems that need resolving.

This monitoring is not intended to replace any of the regular financial information or reports that you have prepared, such as cash flow forecasts or monthly management accounts; it's more to complement these reports and to provide a snapshot of the financial health of your business. Some of the more important monitoring tools are:

- **Debtor days**

  This ratio measures how quickly cash is collected from customers: the higher the figure the longer it takes. If the debtor days ratio is too high, then your credit control

procedure may need looking at. Thirty days is an average benchmark; anything over 45 is likely to have serious cash flow implications for your business. The calculation is as follows:

$$\text{Debtor days} = 365 \times \text{year end (or average debtors) / Sales}$$

The debtor calculation above may need to be adjusted to reflect any applications for payment that may be outstanding.

- **Quick ratio**
  The quick ratio is a measure of how quickly you can convert your cash and liquid assets to meet your liabilities. It is also known as the acid test. The generally accepted benchmark is 1:1 – which means you could use all of your current assets to meet all of your liabilities. The higher the ratio, the greater the liquidity. To calculate this acid test:

  $$\text{Acid Test} = (\text{Cash} + \text{Cash equivalents} + \text{Debtors}) / \text{Liabilities}$$

- **Gearing**
  The gearing ratio measures the financial leverage of a business by comparing the total debt of a company against the amount of equity (the amount the owners have invested, plus retained profits and reserves); the higher the gearing the more vulnerable the business is to trading downturns since it must continue to service debt regardless of sales. A greater proportion of equity provides a cushion and is accepted as a measure of strength. The calculation is shown below:

  $$\text{Gearing} = \text{Debt} / (\text{Debt} + \text{Equity})$$

- **Liquidity**
  This ratio is similar to the quick acid test ratio except it only counts cash and provides a snapshot of liquidity.

A ratio of less than 1:1 means you do not have sufficient cash to meet all of your liabilities. It is calculated as shown:

$$\text{Liquidity} = \text{Cash} / \text{Liabilities}$$

The one-page summary of performance indicators

In our opinion, all businesses could be effectively managed via a one-page summary of the most appropriate KPIs and financial performance indicators. However, for such a summary to be at its most effective, it must be prepared on a regular basis at intervals which will depend on the actual activity of the business: daily, weekly or monthly being the most common. Establishing this performance monitoring framework, including presenting any findings in a clear, succinct and targeted manner will undoubtedly prove beneficial to your business.

Jeffrey Lermer and Karen Wyrwas — Breaking Ground

Cash flow issues

> "Some people dream of success while others wake up and work."
> — *Unknown*

We discussed earlier how the construction industry exhibits a range of special characteristics, and how many of these make the industry a challenging and highly competitive environment in which to operate. This environment exerts considerable pressures on one of the most important aspects of any business – cash flow.

Cash flow is the lifeblood of any business, even more so in the construction industry: low margins, CIS deductions made at source from revenues and other protracted payment methods, retentions, lack of reliable financing options such as factoring or invoice discounting, and a reliance on cash intensive labour and operational costs, all highlight the importance of effective cash flow management. This is before we take into account those external factors that affect the rest of the business world such as bad-paying customers, unhelpful bank managers, demanding suppliers offering poor credit terms – the list is not endless, but can often feel so… and we haven't even mentioned HMRC.

It's difficult to eliminate cash flow pressures entirely since there are many factors that have an impact on cash flow, as well as uncertainties that are, by nature, hard to identify let alone plan for. However, insightful leadership can mitigate some of these pressures through effective cash flow management.

Cash flow management

Managing cash flow is vital for survival and growth, and the first place to start when formulating your cash flow management strategy is by ensuring that you have ready access to accurate and reliable financial information. This information should form the basis of implementing good business practice, and make it easier to take action to help your company avoid a cash crunch.

A summary of proven methods for alleviating or avoiding cash flow issues is shown below.

Preparing cash flow forecasts – Cash flow forecasting can help you plan how much and when to borrow and how much available cash you're likely to have at a given time. Cash flow forecasts are often required to get finance or funding for your business. Accurate cash flow forecasting helps:

- Predict fluctuations in your cash balance
- Work out when you can take on additional financial commitments
- Identify other cash flow problems

Anticipating future problems – Having access to timely financial information and an understanding of the market you operate in can help you to identify and anticipate future problems that may impact your cash flow. Take a proactive approach rather than wait for issues to manifest.

Using working capital effectively – If you've managed to build up a cash reserve, then consider moving it to accounts that pay interest or some other income generating instrument, or using the available cash to pay suppliers early and secure a discount. Liquidity that sits idle is not working for your business.

Controlling costs – It may seem obvious, but keeping costs under control is one of the best defences to stave off potential cash flow issues. Effective leaders have processes in place which regularly monitor costs, allowing them to react more quickly to potential shortfalls in working capital. Sometimes it pays to be draconian, cutting out those unnecessary expenses that eat into cash reserves yet offer little or no tangible benefit. Obviously, some expenditure is essential to the running of your business but belt-tightening never hurt anyone, except perhaps belt manufacturers.

Effective credit control – A failure to keep on top of invoicing and not chasing outstanding customers for payment is a major cause of cash flow problems. Ensure your bookkeeping is well maintained and up to date, and implement a strict credit control policy with terms clearly stated and communicated to customers. Do not hesitate to pursue or escalate the collection process in the event of stubborn customers; if they don't come back for more business, you are probably better off without them. This may not be totally relevant in all cases, since the construction industry can work with differing terms of payment, for example staged payments that may require certification before funds are released – this doesn't mean that the customer cannot be chased though.

Ensuring a high quality of work – Poor standards of work can lead to delays in releasing payment from customers, or even reduce the amount of the payment, if the terms of the contract involve staged applications for payment based on physical work completed. Costs could be incurred in making good defects or other problems, potentially resulting in resources being diverted from other jobs – do not give customers an opportunity to question your work and potentially delay or reduce their remittance.

Keeping tenders realistic – We know the construction industry is highly competitive and it follows that this competitiveness will filter through to any tender process. With such low margins it is arguably better to fail in a bid for work if the terms are too unfavourable. Instead, focus on a robust project-costing process to accurately price jobs so you don't undervalue yourself. Being locked into an undersold contract could have a potentially costly effect for your business.

Maintaining compliance – Put simply, maintaining your statutory obligations can protect you from financial penalties. The construction sector is subject to a strict compliance framework that is underpinned by an unfavourably harsh penalty regime. These penalties can accumulate quite quickly, even for minor infractions. If you are treated as a gross payment business under the CIS, then losing this status and having to suffer a 20% deduction at source for non-compliance could prove disastrous.

Developing good relationships with suppliers – Maintaining good relationships with key suppliers, through communication and ensuring accounts are up to date, can help with obtaining preferential terms and in building credit limits, which can be beneficial during times when cash flow is tight.

Refinancing assets – If you own assets outright, then examining refinancing options such as a sale and leaseback arrangement can help unlock working capital to be used elsewhere.

Exploring finance options – The construction sector is somewhat underserved by access to finance. Options available to other business sectors, such as invoice factoring or discounting, are not forthcoming. However, there are options available and at the very least it pays to maintain a good relationship with your banking provider.

Example: We have managed to secure invoice discounting for construction clients who supply mainly labour services, by agreeing an additional stage in their procedures whereby they obtain signed off timesheets. **Therefore, it may be beneficial to speak to your accountant if you operate in a similar fashion.**

Avoiding overtrading – Overtrading is almost like a business version of 'overenthusiasm'; it involves committing to jobs that you may not necessarily have the resources to complete, whether those resources are liquid or assets. The result is that your working capital may be spread too thinly, leading to problems in finishing jobs and receiving payment. In worst case scenarios, overtrading can prove fatal. You can help prevent overtrading by injecting new capital, acquiring assets using finance lease or HP agreements rather than by paying cash, reducing the amount of money withdrawn from the business and through cost-cutting and efficiency drives.

> **CASE STUDY – Cash flow pressures and scaffolding businesses**
>
> Effective cash flow management is critical for scaffolding businesses. In this sector businesses need to be a member of a large scaffolding association, such as the National Association of Scaffolding Contractors (NASC), in order to be able to compete for large contract jobs. Part of the NASC rules of membership is that at least 90% of scaffolders must be employed, so in order to keep their CIS gross payment status businesses must be fully up to date with their monthly PAYE liabilities.
>
>
>
> This places a great deal of pressure on cash flow, especially as scaffolding businesses have no access to factoring or invoice discounting, so any delays in valuations and payments are likely to have serious consequences. Furthermore, scaffolders need to spend a fortune on scaffolding kit, and this needs to be paid for promptly.
>
> *Therefore, you need to be very well funded and have effective cash management procedures in place to be able to run a big scaffolding business.*

Jeffrey Lermer and Karen Wyrwas

9

Outline of the Construction Industry Scheme

> "You can't change the direction of the wind, but you can adjust the direction of your sail to help you reach your destination."
>
> — *Anon*

The construction industry is governed by a special regulatory framework known as the Construction Industry Scheme (CIS), and this framework is one of the unique characteristics of the overall sector. Like most regulatory edicts, the CIS is highly susceptible to change as the authorities look to iron out potential problems and close any loopholes. This propensity to 'sea change' has seen a major evolution within the sector over the past few decades, and it is worth taking a moment to study the progression of the various schemes over time in order to gain some level of insight into the overall objectives of HMRC in respect of the industry. A more detailed look at CIS in its present form will hopefully help you to understand and appreciate the finer details and nuances of the scheme, ensuring your business is well-equipped to react to any fundamental changes which may quite possibly affect the industry in coming years.

A brief history of construction industry schemes

The construction industry is a highly competitive market, yet it suffers from low margins. The original construction industry scheme, introduced in 1971, was known as the Construction Industry Tax Deduction Scheme (CITDS) and was an attempt by the Treasury to ensure it received the correct dues from what was perceived to be an itinerant sector that sought to exploit loopholes to alleviate the problems of these continually low margins. The primary concern at the time, and perhaps still now, was that workers were often incorrectly categorised as self-employed, which ultimately led to a loss of tax revenue for the authorities, whilst adding – what some perceived to be – beneficial cost savings for those who used these workers' services. The CITDS ensured that subcontractors were paid with a deduction of 30%, and given an SC60 certificate which documented the deduction, whilst exemption certificates were given to subcontractors who were eligible, i.e. those with a good compliance history. All things considered, it was a very paper-heavy process, with a vast number of certificates and vouchers flying around, and as with any such complex scheme, the opportunities for non-compliance were huge. Despite this, the CITDS ran for over 20 years with just a few minor tweaks and changes until developing technologies made the scheme look tired, cumbersome and inefficient, and it was not seen to be achieving its original aims with any certainty.

As well as proving incredibly cumbersome for businesses to manage and operate, the CITDS was failing to address a fundamental concern of HMRC, namely that a significant number of workers were being wrongly classified as self-employed when they were actually working under terms that could clearly be defined as employment. This was creating a loss of revenue for the government, and therefore a new scheme was needed. Enter the CIS, developed in 1995 and introduced in 1999. The CIS required more work from those engaged in the building industry; the first such requirement was the need for all contractors to review and, where appropriate, to correct the employment status of workers. Subcontractors themselves were required to register with HMRC in order to receive payment for work in construction – a clear message of 'no card, no pay' was intended to deter non-compliance and assist the authorities in tracking all payments made within the construction industry. Subcontractors were faced with two levels of certification: CIS4 and CIS6/CIS5.

CIS4 – Often called the 'net payment certificate', enabled its bearer to be paid for construction work but with the contractor required to deduct an 18% retention for tax purposes on the labour element of any invoice. This deduction was evidenced by a monthly payment certificate which the subcontractor used when preparing his end-of-year accounts or tax returns, reclaiming any excess tax deduction retained and remitted to HMRC by the contractor during the year.

CIS6 and CIS5 – Certain subcontractors were granted gross payment status evidenced by a CIS6 or CIS5 certificate. This status was highly desirable, not only because it meant that payment could be received without any immediate deduction, but many commercial contracts were only issued to holders of CIS6 or CIS5 certificates. To qualify for a CIS6 card a subcontractor needed to pass three tests:

- **The turnover test**
  Subcontractors trading as an individual needed to demonstrate their net turnover from construction work, excluding materials, exceeded £30,000 per year, and this figure must have been attained for a continuous period of three years immediately before the date that the CIS6 card was applied for. Where the subcontractor was trading in partnership or as a limited company, this £30,000 annual requirement applied to each partner or director, so a small company with five directors needed to demonstrate an annual turnover of £150,000 in order to be eligible for a CIS6 card.

- **The business test**
  This required the subcontractor to run their affairs in a business-like manner; essentially operating with a business bank account and maintaining proper business records. In short, evidence of a properly run business needed to be maintained.

- **The compliance test**
  The gross payment certificates required renewal in three-yearly intervals, and over these intervals the subcontractors must have paid all tax, including PAYE and subcontractor deductions, and submitted all tax returns on time.
  Failure to meet these requirements would, in most cases, constitute a failure of the compliance test.

Given that these CIS6 and CIS5 certificates were issued with a three-year lifespan, there was ample opportunity for HMRC to verify these three tests and evaluate the compliance record of businesses, but criticism was often levelled at the inconsistent approach of differing tax offices in deciding which minor and technical failures led to a revocation of CIS6 and CIS5 cards. As one would expect, any loss of gross payment certificate understandably proved difficult for many businesses to handle.

Despite the improvements over the CITDS system, this new system still failed to alleviate the administrative burden on construction businesses, with the continued reliance on physical vouchers issued between contractors and subcontractors, ensuring that huge volumes of paperwork were still being generated. Above all, from HMRC's perspective, it failed to completely redress the confusion and compliance surrounding the employment status of workers.

The present CIS

The CIS we know today was introduced almost ten years ago, in 2007. Since this time it has undergone a few minor evolutions, mostly as a reaction to the effect that evolving technologies have had on recording and reporting information to HMRC. The scope of the CIS is wide ranging and encompasses the following:

- The jurisdiction of the scheme
- The definition of 'contractors' and 'subcontractors'
- Contracts for construction operations and 'contract payments'
- The meaning of 'construction operations'
- Observations on the direct costs of materials

Jurisdiction

The CIS applies to any **construction operations** undertaken within the UK, or within 12 miles of its territorial waters. It is important to note that it is the type of operation that decides whether the CIS is applicable, and not the entity that is carrying out the operation. Also, residency has no effect; non-UK resident activities fall within the scope of CIS so long as the operations are carried out in the UK.

Contractors

In general terms, a contractor is a person, or entity, that enters into a contract with another person, or entity, to carry out construction operations. They can generally be defined as being one of two groups: mainstream or deemed.

Mainstream contractors are any person, body or organisation that is carrying on a business which includes construction operations. Essentially, this means that if construction activity is a fundamental part of a business, then that business will be a mainstream contractor for the purposes of the CIS. There is no minimum level of expenditure on construction operations before registration is required; it is the fundamental association with construction that forces this registration.

Deemed contractors are somewhat different in that they are broadly defined as those businesses whose core business activity is not construction related, but who nonetheless exceed a minimum level of expenditure on construction operations. This expenditure level is presently set at an average £1m per year measured over three years, although CIS will trigger as soon as the whole three-year sum, i.e. £3m, is reached – so, if you are a non-construction business that spends £3.5m on construction operations over an 18-month period, then you will fall within the scope of CIS for these construction activities, in addition to meeting any usual business reporting obligations.

This level of expenditure also applies when a transfer of trade occurs. So when a business acquires another business then any portion of expenditure on construction operations is also transferred, for the purposes of assessing the requirement for operating the CIS within the three-year, £1m per year guidelines.

Remember, under the CIS it is the sole responsibility of the contractor to ensure that legislation is followed – failure to do so may trigger financial penalties, or, in worse cases, affect the payment status of the contractor.

Once registered as a contractor for CIS purposes, you must continue to operate within the scheme until there are three consecutive years of less than £1m annual expenditure on construction operations. The onus is on you to satisfy HMRC that you no longer meet the requirements for CIS.

Subcontractors

Whenever there is a contract for construction operations, then a subcontractor is defined as:

- Any person or entity that is under duty to a contractor to carry out construction operations regardless of whether they, in carrying out the construction operations, provide their own labour, the labour of their employees, or the labour of any other person
- Any person or entity that is answerable to a contractor for the construction operations that are carried out by others

The important point to note here is that the person or entity **must be under a duty** to carry out the construction works, or be **answerable** to a contractor. Furthermore, where a subcontractor chooses to subcontract part or all of the work to a third party, they will also be classified as a contractor for the purposes of CIS, and will be required to operate CIS in respect of any payments made to third parties.

Currently there are three types of subcontractors under the CIS:

- Those that can be paid gross without any deduction
- Those that can be paid with a standard deduction of 20%
- Those paid with a higher deduction of 30%

Contractors must make these specific deductions from the payments made to subcontractors where the payments are contract payments, i.e. any payment made under a contract for construction operations.

A grey area exists around the work of certain professionals in the building trade, for example architects, surveyors or consultants. Traditionally, these professionals have been excluded from the scope of the CIS on the basis that most of their duties are of a consultative basis such as drawing plans, inspecting land, etc. However, over recent years the sort of work carried out by such professionals has broadened to the extent that, **in some cases**, some of the services could be sufficient for them to be classified as **subcontractors.** In general, if the work carried out by these professionals takes on a more executive approach, for example project managing a construction job or overseeing its day-to-day execution, then they would fall within the chain of command between the person carrying out the work – the subcontractor – and the main contractor, and would therefore be acting as a subcontractor for the purposes of CIS.

Contract for construction operations

It is common knowledge that a contract need not be in writing; verbal or implied agreements are also sufficient under UK law. Regardless of whether a contract is written or otherwise, it must be for construction operations for the work undertaken to fall within the scope of the CIS. Care must be taken, however, since some contracts may be ambiguous with respect to the extent of construction operations – in general, if any component of a contract, however small, is for construction operations, then **all** work under that contract is deemed to fall within the CIS. Note that any failure to operate the CIS could leave you exposed with potential liabilities to tax, interest and penalties, so seeking appropriate advice is recommended.

Contract payments

A contract payment is any payment made by a contractor, under a contract for construction, to a subcontractor (or someone nominated by the subcontractor). Some payments made by contractors in respect of construction operations are not counted as contract payments, for example:

- Payments made to an employee, where the payment is treated under PAYE
- Payments made to subcontractors who are registered with HMRC and entitled to be paid without deduction, or payments made to a nominee, where the person nominating is also entitled to be paid without deduction (gross payment status)

The whole concept of contract payments is to define simply the type of payment from which a deduction under CIS must be made – in other words, payments made to gross payment subcontractors do not indicate that they are outside the scope of the CIS.

Construction operations

Understanding which types of operations are within the scope of the CIS is one of the most complicated issues facing contractors. The lines between activities can often be blurred; for example, fitting carpets is never classified as a construction operation, whereas fitting another type of floor covering may be. In general, the term 'construction operations' covers the following:

- Any work that is done to a permanent or temporary building or structure
- Civil engineering work and installation

This means that construction operations include the construction, alteration, repair, extension and demolition of:

- Buildings and structures, including offshore installations
- Any works forming part of the land including walls, roadworks, power lines, electronic communications apparatus, runways, docks, railways, inland waterways, reservoirs, wells, sewers and industrial plants

It may further include:

- The installation in any building or structure of systems of heating, lighting, air conditioning, ventilation, power supply, sewerage, sanitation, water supply or fire protection
- Internal cleaning of buildings if undertaken as part of a process of construction, alteration, repair, extension or demolition
- Painting or decorating the external or internal structure of any building
- Any other operations that are an integral part of the preparatory or completion processes involved with any of the above mentioned activities, such as site clearing, excavation, tunnelling, laying foundations, erection of scaffolding, landscaping and the provision of transport infrastructure or other access works

The scope of construction operations is clearly very broad and, on the whole, fairly logical in its definition – **if the work alters or changes the structure of a building (whether permanent or temporary) then it is likely to be defined as a construction operation.**

A few grey areas exist, mostly in the area of installation, such as work which involves security systems, wiring, blinds or shutters. In most cases, these fall outside the scope of CIS unless during its installation it requires alteration of the existing building, for example installing new ducting to carry wires rather than using existing ones. A final point to be aware of involves mixed contracts, i.e. contracts which involve operations that are both within and outside the HMRC definition of construction operations. In such cases, the **whole** contract is treated as falling within the CIS.

Direct costs of materials

The final point to make is in regard of the cost of materials. Traditionally, under the CIS, the cost of materials that subcontractors suffer is exempt from any deduction; it is only the labour element that forms the starting point for the various levels of deduction. This rule only applies, however, to the direct cost of materials; any margin you add in recharging the expenditure on materials to customers becomes liable for deduction as well. For example, if your labour costs are £500 and you charge a £100 premium for materials that physically cost you £200, then your amount liable for CIS deduction is £600, i.e. the £500 labour plus the £100 mark-up on the direct cost of materials. It is the responsibility of the contractor to verify that the cost of materials exempted from deduction is correct. There are some unscrupulous subcontractors who will claim higher costs for materials to reduce their CIS deduction. HMRC are aware of this practice and will raise an enquiry into the contractor's affairs if they suspect that the contractor is declaring unfeasibly high costs of materials in the payments made to subcontractors.

The contractor must be able to demonstrate that the materials element of all invoices paid by them has been thoroughly checked and will have to pay over additional CIS deductions and penalties if they cannot satisfy HMRC in this regard.

Operating the CIS

Operating the CIS is somewhat easier than it has been historically, but it still imparts a considerable administrative burden on businesses. Luckily, technology and software can help alleviate this burden, and many powerful packages are available that can assist with the monthly reporting and other compliance requirements associated with the scheme.

A basic requirement, as we established, is that contractors must register with HMRC in order to operate the scheme; likewise, subcontractors must also register in order to avoid higher rates of deduction (30% instead of the standard 20%). Once registered, contractors are obliged to submit a regular monthly CIS return, which details all payments made to all subcontractors (regardless of their legal status, i.e. sole traders or limited companies) throughout each payment month, with these reporting periods running from the 6th of the previous month to the 5th of the following.

Verification

Before any payments can be made to a subcontractor, the contractor must 'verify' them with HMRC. This verification process involves contacting HMRC and providing details of the subcontractor, typically National Insurance number, UTR number, company registration number (if applicable), as well as a contact address. The easiest method for obtaining subcontractor verification is via an online EDI, either through a dedicated HMRC website or, more preferably, through recognised payroll software programs.

This information is used by HMRC to verify the payment status of the subcontractor, and details will be sent back stipulating one of the three levels of deduction: 20%, 30% or no deduction, together with a Verification Number (VRN) which will need to be noted, either in the software package used or when submitting the CIS returns through HMRC portals. In the event of insufficient information being provided to HMRC, for example failing to provide a valid UTR number, the default setting will be at 30% until the subcontractor is fully registered with HMRC or further information is supplied.

Obviously, it is in the interest of subcontractors to ensure that they are correctly registered with HMRC and they provide all necessary information to the contractor in order to avoid higher rates of deduction.

The payment status deduction rate issued by HMRC must never be overridden.

Making payments

Once subcontractors are verified, and correct deduction rates are applied, then payments can be made. Deductions at the relevant rates are made net of VAT and exclude the direct cost of materials, and are also made after any retentions or CITB levies have been applied. The contractor is also expected to check any element classified as 'materials' to ensure it has not been overstated by the subcontractor in order to reduce the deduction of tax.

Issuing statements

The requirement to issue vouchers to subcontractors on a monthly basis has disappeared; however, contractors are required to issue statements detailing the gross payment amount (including VAT), the cost of materials and the amount of tax deducted, as well as specifying the particulars of both contractor and subcontractor (UTRs, employers reference, etc.). These statements must be issued no later than 14 days after the month they refer to. Most payroll or bookkeeping software programs offer statement functionality.

Payments made to subcontractors by credit card

In the unlikely event of making a payment to a subcontractor using a credit card, perhaps because of cash flow problems, there may exist timing differences between when the subcontractor receives payment and when the contractor physically makes the actual repayment to the credit card provider. The treatment, and subsequent reporting date to HMRC, is dependent on the exact accounting system of the contractor, i.e. when he recognises that payment has been made, which may be in the following month.

Example – Calculating CIS deductions

The following is an example of a calculation where materials and labour have been supplied, and the main contractor has paid the subcontractor's expenses.

A tiling subcontractor, who is not VAT registered, agrees to tile a bathroom and to provide all materials for a total payment of £540. The materials have cost the subcontractor £240 (which is £200 + £40 VAT). The contractor agrees to pay £50 fuel expenses.

	£
Labour charge	300
Materials	240
Fuel	50
Amount due (invoice amount)	**590**
Calculation of deduction	
Amount due	590
Less cost of materials (inc. VAT)	−240
Amount liable for deduction	350
CIS tax deducted at 20%	−70
Net payment to subcontractor	**520**

The contractor deducts the cost of the materials from the price for the whole job and calculates the deduction on the difference (£350). If the subcontractor was registered for VAT then the deduction would be based on the difference between the total payment, excluding VAT, less the price of materials excluding VAT.

Payments to HMRC

If the contractor is also an employer, then any deductions from payments made to subcontractors must be paid to the HMRC Accounts Office with the normal monthly PAYE/National

Insurance Contribution (NIC) deduction. If the monthly payments average less than £1,500, then payments can be made quarterly. There are deadlines in place for when payments must reach HMRC in order to avoid surcharges:

- The 22nd of the month following – if paid electronically
- The 19th of the month following – if paid otherwise

CIS offsets

Limited companies are allowed to offset CIS deductions they have suffered against amounts they owe to HMRC in respect of CIS and PAYE deductions the company withholds from its own employees or CIS subcontractors. This facility is **not** available to sole traders or LLPs. If the situation arises where a company's own deductions are greater than their ongoing monthly payments in respect of PAYE, NIC, Student Loan and CIS deductions, then any excess can be offset against future monthly payments within that same tax year; this is typically done in collaboration with their usual monthly reporting requirements as an employer, known as an Employer Payment Submission (EPS). At the end of the tax year, companies are required to submit end-of-year returns for their payroll, and any excess of deductions suffered can be either refunded to the company or offset against another tax liability, such as corporation tax or VAT. This must be requested in writing to HMRC, otherwise the excess is simply credited to the PAYE account.

For sole traders or partnerships, credit for CIS tax suffered must be claimed on the annual personal tax return of the respective sole trader or partner. In limited cases, where the accounting period ends part way through the tax year and the total deductions exceed the expected tax bill, then a refund can be claimed by submission of a CIS40 (sole traders) or CIS41 (LLPs).

Statutory returns

Every month, contractors are obliged to submit a CIS return (or CIS300) to HMRC summarising all the payments made to subcontractors during the 'tax' month, which runs from the 6th of one month to the 5th of the subsequent month. This must be submitted electronically to HMRC by the 19th of the following month. As well as full details of the subcontractor payments, including the breakdown of the materials costs and the CIS tax deducted, the contractor must confirm on the CIS return the following:

- **Verification declaration** – all subcontractors have been verified and the correct deduction rate has been applied
- **Status declaration** – the contractor has verified the employment status of subcontractors

As with most returns to HMRC, penalties are liable for failure to submit on time. These penalties rapidly increase in severity, the later the return is submitted.

Real Time Information (RTI)

Payroll, including CIS, operates in real time, with employers required to submit Full Payment Submissions (FPS) each month, and an EPS. These regular submissions manage the reporting of employee details including leavers and starters, payments and PAYE/NI deductions. The EPS also reports CIS offset deductions for limited companies, making it easier for companies to reclaim deductions they've suffered and counter their regular PAYE/NI/CIS liabilities.

Errors on returns

You should ensure that the monthly CIS return reflects all the payments made to subcontractors during a particular month. However, it is almost inevitable that errors will occur.

If the filing deadline has not passed – simply repair the data and resubmit the return. HMRC may subsequently write to you asking which of the two CIS returns is the correct one.

If the filing deadline has passed – contact the CIS Helpline to inform HMRC of the errors and to agree the best procedure to correct the submitted return.

Underpayments or overpayments made – where the error relates to incorrect payments, you can make a balancing payment in the following month, either by increasing or reducing the subsequent payment. One point to note is that balancing payments can only be made within the same tax year.

Jeffrey Lermer and Karen Wyrwas

The future of the Construction Industry Scheme

> "Success is not the key to happiness. Happiness is the key to success. If you love what you are doing, you will be successful."
> — *Albert Schweitzer*

The construction industry has faced tough times over recent years with the wounds of the recession taking a long time to heal, and the overall economic climate stifling growth. The attitude of the tax authorities towards the industry, perhaps pressurised by austerity measures and the need to protect public finances, is difficult to predict, but it seems fairly certain that all businesses will face greater scrutiny and statutory obligations in the future. Part of this is being driven by technology, with regular EDI between businesses and HMRC heralding a new era of transparency and digital government. Plans are already in place for submission of self-assessment, corporation tax and other business returns to transition to a more regular, electronic format. This huge exchange of data will allow HMRC to more effectively monitor business compliance.

There exists a real possibility that HMRC will seek to utilise the rapid exchange of information and advances in technologies to develop the existing Construction Industry Scheme (CIS) into something that may look entirely different. Obviously, the impact of such an evolution is difficult to predict given it lies in the future, but we can examine recent consultation documents to get a flavour of the thought processes of the authorities; the current CIS, introduced in 2007, arose out of a 2002 consultation document, so historically these have proven a fairly accurate benchmark for future legislation.

The future may be bright, but we recommend sunglasses rather than rose-tinted spectacles...

Recent consultation documents

In 2009 the HM Treasury and HMRC jointly issued a consultation document entitled 'False self-employment in construction: taxation of workers'. As the title suggests, the document once again raised the bugbear of the employment status of workers across the construction sector, and proposed to adopt an industry-specific test, for taxation purposes, in order to address the perceived problem.

Much like a broken record, the document suggested that the differences between employed and self-employed gave workers, and those that engaged them, a financial incentive and benefit to portray employment income as self-employed income. This comes despite the introduction of the current CIS in 2007, which had this issue of employment status as a central tenet, since which time there has been little proven case law of a construction worker's status being overturned in favour of HMRC.

Despite this, the 2009 consultation proposed three criteria tests which it considers as a reliable indicator of employment status:

- **Provision of plant and machinery** – the worker provides the plant and machinery required to complete the job
- **Provision of all materials** – the worker provides all material required to complete a job, and
- **Provision of other workers** – the worker provides other workers to carry out work under contract and is responsible for paying them

Workers will have to meet at least one of these to be classed as self-employed.

The benefits to HMRC from adopting this approach is clear – increased tax revenues. Another potential benefit is that, on the face of it, the three criteria seem quite explicit and easy to understand; this may lead to a reduction in the cost of policing compliance.

The impact on workers and contractors are likely to be less beneficial. It would likely lead to downward pressure on wages, as subcontractors on variable hours might be replaced by full-time employees on lower hourly rates. Some self-employed workers might also lose the various tax advantages and benefits of being self-employed. For contractors, it is clear that a whole new administrative burden will materialise, undoubtedly with a severe penalty regime for non-compliance. Most important of all is that employment status is not an issue that is confined to the construction sector, but it appears that the construction industry gets all the attention from the authorities, thereby eroding trust and fostering an environment of mistrust and non-compliance.

To date, there has been no further movement from the government in respect of this consultation document, although this is not in itself unusual since the time lapse between consultation documents and final legislation can be very lengthy.

Tellingly, a further consultation report was published in December 2013, snappily entitled 'Onshore Employment Intermediaries: False Self-Employment' and, although not aimed specifically at the construction sector, over 80% of its contents were primarily directed at the employment status of workers in construction. Much like its predecessor, the 2013 documents outlined two tests to verify the status of workers: a **control** test; and a **personal provision of services** test. The first is self-evident – the worker exerts control over the job he is engaged to do and this 'control' may include how it is done, when it is done, or what materials are used, etc.; but the second is more ambiguous: a worker could arrange a substitute to carry out the work, and this could be argued to represent a personal provision of services.

No one can predict with any certainty how the CIS landscape will look in the future; however, one thing that is certain is the apparent determination of HMRC to continue in its pursuit of the perceived non-compliant construction sector. This determination appears to have gained support through the implementation of new technologies to assist in the exchange of information between businesses, individuals and government. As the information businesses are required to report becomes more real time and accessible, the authorities will possess greater and more powerful tools to monitor businesses and enforce compliance. In light of this, one hopes that HMRC takes a more inclusive approach to its particular issue with the construction industry, and works with construction businesses to develop a robust, easy to implement and effective CIS framework.

What can you do?

It may not be possible to second guess the future and make adequate preparations against what is generally a moving target, but it still doesn't hurt to appreciate how the authorities view your industry and to gain some insight into what their primary objectives are. It is clear that the CIS will evolve, sooner rather than later; after all, the last revision was almost ten years ago, and the world is now a very different, more interconnected place than it was then. If you accept this eventuality and take the following proactive steps, then any new introduction might be less painful to absorb:

- Ensuring that records are well maintained
- Meeting all compliance obligations
- Keeping all accounting and bookkeeping software up to date so any transition to further online filing requirements, however regular, is seamless
- Increase the industry and compliance knowledge base amongst key staff through regular training
- Communicate regularly with your accountant and professional advisors
- Monitor relevant HMRC news feeds and consultation documents

Extracting remuneration

> "Success seems to be connected with action. Successful people keep moving. They make mistakes, but they don't quit."
>
> — *Conrad Hilton*

The primary reason for commencing trade or establishing a business is with a view to making profit. And for the owners of a business, subsequently taking a share of this profit is of fundamental importance; after all, there's no point running a profitable business if you can't enjoy the fruits of your labour.

For those construction businesses that are incorporated as LLPs or self-employed partnerships or sole traders, extracting remuneration is fairly straightforward since most monies are drawn from such legal entities without any attached tax implications; any tax liability is instead associated with the actual profit the business makes. However, for limited companies, the rules for extracting profits are different, as are the implications for tax.

Each limited company needs to be examined on its own merit, and specific circumstances need to be taken into account. This is where a good relationship with your accountant helps, as they will undoubtedly have a keen grasp of your business activities and will probably offer assistance in constructing effective remuneration packages as part of their service to you.

Below is a brief summary of some of the more familiar methods of withdrawing money from a limited company:

1. **Remuneration** – This means payments such as wages, salaries, bonuses, etc. that are taxed by HMRC as employment income. Providing you are a director or employee of a company, these payments are an allowable deduction against the corporation tax liability of the company. Effectively, if the company makes £100,000 profit, and you pay remuneration to yourself of £20,000, as a basic example, then the £20,000 'profit', or salary, you have withdrawn has no corporation tax liability.

Instead, there exists an income tax liability for the person receiving this payment, the amount of which is dependent on their total income for that particular tax year. In addition, employee's National Insurance at 12% is deductible on salary paid above the primary threshold (£671 per month in 2016/17). A further tax burden is borne in the form of employer's National Insurance, a 'tax' that is currently levied at 13.8% on all salaries paid above the secondary threshold (£676 per month in 2016/17). Remuneration isn't therefore a low-cost option.

2. **Dividends** – Shareholders in limited companies can be entitled to dividends, which are payments made out of profits. Unlike remuneration, dividends are not an allowable deduction against corporation tax liability. The rules for dividends changed in April 2016, and they are no longer considered as being received net of a 10% tax credit. Instead, an annual dividend allowance of £5,000 is awarded tax free, with additional tax rates applying depending on which tax band they fall into:

- 7.5% on dividend income within the basic rate band
- 32.5% on dividend income within the higher rate band
- 38.1% on dividend income within the additional rate band

The new rules slightly increase the tax costs of dividends, as the following examples highlight, but despite this, dividends may be more efficient, especially for family companies where a number of family members participate and receive dividends.

2016/17 new rules example: the dividend allowance is within your basic rate tax band

If you are **a basic rate taxpayer**, you receive a small salary of £11,000 to use up your personal tax free allowance and the remainder of your taxable income as dividends. **You will have a personal tax liability of £2,025.**

The basic rate tax threshold for 2016/17 is £43,000 (personal allowance of £11,000, plus basic rate tax band of £32,000).

If a dividend of £32,000 is received it is taxable as follows, breaking it down into the different 'slices':

The first £5,000 – covered by your tax free dividend allowance.

The next £27,000 (the remainder of your basic rate band) – taxed at the new 7.5% = £2,025 tax due.

Under the old rules (if they were in place in 2016/17)

If a dividend of £32,000 is paid as above, the gross taxable dividend (accounting for the 10% tax credit) would be £35,555. Of this, £32,000 would have no further tax payable. The balance of £3,555 would have an additional 22.5% tax liability (32.5% less the 10% already credited), so £800 tax due.

Example: Dividends for higher rate taxpayers

A higher rate taxpayer pays tax at 32.5% on any dividend income in excess of the new £5,000 dividend allowance and basic rate threshold, and an upper rate taxpayer will be taxed at the new 38.1% rate.

If you are a **higher rate taxpayer**, and you receive £50,000 of income in dividends in 2016/17, **you will be worse off by £2,575.**

If a dividend of £50,000 is received it is taxable as follows, breaking it down into the different 'slices':

The first £5,000 – covered by your dividend allowance

The next £27,000 – taxed at the new 7.5% = £2,025

The next £18,000 – taxed at 32.5%   = £5,850

Total tax due   = £7,875

Re-working 2016/17 for a higher rate tax payer (for illustration only – old rules)

If a dividend of £50,000 is received that is grossed up to £55,555 it is taxable as follows, breaking it down into the different 'slices':

The first £32,000 – taxed at 10%	= £3,200
The next £23,555 – taxed at 32.5%	= £7,655
You receive a tax credit	= £ (5,555)
Total tax due	**= £5,300**

The above examples assume that the taxpayer has other income which takes up their personal allowance.

3. **Interest** – If you funded the company by means of a director's loan through its formative years, then there is no reason why the company shouldn't pay interest – at a fair, commercial rate – on that loan. This interest payment could then become a form of profit extraction. The tax treatment is similar to remuneration, in that the company gains an allowable deduction on the interest paid, but unlike remuneration there is no National Insurance charge. Interest paid by a company to an individual must be paid net of 20% tax, as banks did until 5th April 2016 (banks now pay interest gross, without deduction of tax). The company must notify HMRC of any interest paid to UK resident individuals on a quarterly basis using a CT61 form, and the 20% tax deducted must be paid to HMRC at the same time.

4. **Rent** – Similarly to interest, if you run the company and own the premises from which the company trades, you could charge the company a rent (or allow them the premises rent free!) If you charge a rent that is in line with a fair market value, then this becomes another method of extracting profit that is allowable for corporation tax

deduction, as well as avoiding a National Insurance charge. One potential hurdle to this method is the new capital gains tax (CGT) rules for Entrepreneurs' Relief, which, if you sold both business and property at the same time, could result in a significantly higher CGT payable in respect of the property.

5. **Loans** – The basic premise here is that you arrange for the company to lend you money. Be aware that when a director borrows money from a private company this is no longer considered as illegal, but if the loan amount exceeds £10,000, the director must have secured shareholder approval. If the loan to a director remains outstanding nine months after the company's accounting year ends, then HMRC will enforce 32.5% of the loan value as a temporary tax charge to the company (this tax charge will be refunded to the company nine months after the accounting year in which it is repaid by the director). So loans to directors can be effective if the 'loan' is repaid within nine months following the year end, although some benefit in kind liability may arise if there is not sufficient interest charged on the director by the company.

6. **Selling assets to the company** – To take advantage of lower CGT, you could sell an asset to the company, for example a property you own, or even the goodwill of a business that you are putting into the company.

Providing the amount the company pays you is a fair market price, then you can receive payment out of the company without being subject to any tax higher than the relevant CGT rate.

7. **Liquidation** – The most drastic form of extracting profits is to liquidate the company. If the company counts as a trading company for the purposes of Entrepreneurs' Relief, then you will have no more than 10% tax to pay, because liquidation proceeds are subject to CGT and its associated reliefs (such as Entrepreneurs' Relief) and not income tax. However, liquidation is quite a serious step that is not without consequence, so professional advice is always recommended. Furthermore, new legislation prevents serial liquidations, so this is more of a one-off profit extraction method for when you no longer wish to trade in the construction sector.

There are other methods of extracting remuneration from businesses, some of which are fairly technical and more aggressive than others. These types of 'schemes' have drawn considerable press attention, following some high-profile cases through the courts. In general, they are considered 'risky' and potentially 'morally wrong'.

Notwithstanding those more specialist packages, it helps to ask a few simple questions when comparing differing methods of extracting profits from a limited company:

1. How is this remuneration going to impact the tax liability of the company?

2. What will be the tax implications from a personal perspective?

3. Will the amount of remuneration have a negative effect on the cash flow of the company?

Cash flow is vital for businesses, not only for growth in the future, but also for maintaining current operations. You may feel the need to limit your level of remuneration in order to ensure your working capital is not adversely affected – after all, future profits may be higher and be able to support higher levels of remuneration. Having said that, many tax reliefs are lost if not used within a certain tax year, so it does become something of a balancing act.

Sitting down with your accountant, and working through your needs and other financial circumstances – perhaps with a careful eye on the future – is probably the best course of action in developing an optimal remuneration package that maximises the benefits of annual tax reliefs, is most effective from a corporate tax perspective, and doesn't negatively impact working capital.

12 Assets

> "A company's greatest asset is its people."
> — *Henry Ford*

Henry Ford was probably right: a company's greatest asset is its people. But, if these people have no equipment, machinery, tools or vehicles to operate, then your construction business is likely to suffer. If you work in the construction sector, the chances are you already own, or are likely to need in the future, assets. These assets may be relatively inexpensive, for example a small van, or they may be much greater in scope, such as a fleet of trucks or a piece of heavy plant machinery like an excavator. The truth is the construction sector is highly dependent on a whole range of equipment, plant, machinery and vehicles, and regardless of the size of your business, you will undoubtedly need some 'assets' to help you deliver your services.

Accounting for assets

From an accounting perspective, assets are classified as a capital expense and treated as balance sheet items; this means that they have a tangible (in most cases, at least) value, which is written off over a period of time against your income. Tax relief, in the form of capital allowances, is available to encourage businesses to invest and to offset the cost of purchasing assets. In most cases, the full cost of an asset can be deducted from profits before tax is calculated by using the Annual Investment Allowance (AIA). For 2016, the AIA limit is £200,000 – meaning that eligible assets purchased up to this total can be offset immediately; exceptions include cars, leased assets and buildings, although certain fixtures and fittings do qualify. In the case of these exceptions, a lower 'writing down allowance' (WDA) of either 8% or 18% may be used, depending on the exact type of asset.

We can agree that generous tax reliefs for investing in assets is a good thing and, obviously, forward-looking businesses need to be adequately equipped to be able to deliver their services, and this requires regular investment in plant and machinery to replace obsolete, old or malfunctioning assets. The problem being is that we saw earlier how the construction sector suffers from low margins, which can contribute to cash flow pressures, making it difficult to access readily the necessary funds to invest in plant and machinery. So it almost becomes a catch-22 situation: you need working capital to invest in the new plant and machinery to drive growth, but you need growth to increase working capital.

In this chapter, therefore, we will take a quick look at some of the options that are available to businesses to acquire and own assets, highlighting the relative benefits, or downsides, associated with each.

Self-purchase

The most obvious method of owning an asset is to buy it outright. Simple. You pay for the asset, and perhaps purchase some additional warranty or servicing agreement to go alongside, and you own it outright. The business gains some 'value' on its balance sheet, and no doubt benefits from tax relief, either for one year (in the case of AIA) or over a period of time through WDAs. The main problem of an outright purchase is the upfront cost; of course, you might secure a better deal, advantageous in the long run, but there may be a consequential cash flow impact. For this reason, unless businesses are extremely cash rich, buying an asset outright is probably much more suitable for smaller, inexpensive items.

Asset finance

Asset finance is a collective term which describes a more flexible approach to funding that offers businesses access to plant, machinery, vehicles or other assets without compromising on cash flow. It can apply to the purchase of new or second-hand assets, or even refer to a mechanism for releasing funds from assets that you may already own. The flexible approach means that it has become one of the fastest-growing financing options for businesses of all sizes to acquire and operate the equipment they need.

The four most readily available types of asset finance are:

- Hire purchase
- Finance lease
- Operating lease
- Refinance

Hire purchase (HP)

Most people are familiar with HP, which is a flexible method of acquiring an asset whilst paying for it in instalments over a specified time period, making it easier to budget finances and proving more flexible than securing a conventional loan. At the end of this time period there exists an option to buy the asset outright. This method is particularly useful for acquiring vehicles, machinery or equipment, especially those assets that may have a resale value following the end of the term. The benefits of HP are fairly self-explanatory:

- Allows the cost of purchase to be spread over time
- Tax efficient, with any HP interest being offset against pre-tax profits, and as the owner of the asset it may qualify for capital allowances
- The VAT is reclaimable on the capital cost of the asset, although special rules apply for cars

Finance lease

A finance lease is similar to HP in that regular instalments are paid, but at the end of the agreement the asset is not owned outright. Essentially, the asset is rented from a finance company, who allow full use of the equipment during the lease period, with the full cost of the asset (typically vehicles) being paid plus interest. At the end of the lease term, the asset can continue to be used under a cheaper, secondary rental period; or returned to the finance company; or sold, with a portion of the sale proceeds being kept by you. Benefits of finance leasing include:

- Greater flexibility as instalment and rental repayments can often be tailored to suit your own specific cash flow needs
- Low initial outlay, i.e. often a smaller deposit than with HP
- Tax efficient with monthly rentals usually eligible to be offset against pre-tax profits
- Potential cash-back sum if the asset is sold at the end of the finance lease agreement
- VAT on monthly rentals can be reclaimed, although restrictions may apply for certain vehicles

Operating lease

An operating lease allows you to rent an asset whilst you need it. This generally means you are renting an asset over only a part of its expected useful lifetime and therefore the monthly rental payments are lower than those associated with a finance lease, since at the end of the term the asset is not owned by you but will still possess a residual value to the finance company. At the end of the lease, the asset can either be re-rented or returned. Core benefits of this method of asset finance are:

- Freedom to use an asset without the added burden of disposing of or owning the asset at the end of the operating lease

- A low initial capital outlay
- Low monthly rentals compared to a finance lease, since cost is based on a percentage value of the asset, rather than the whole
- VAT on monthly rentals can be reclaimed, although restrictions may apply for certain vehicles

Refinance

Refinance is a different type of asset finance that allows businesses to unlock the value of assets that they already own, and is a particularly effective way of releasing working capital to ease cash flow problems or to reinvest into new assets. The most common form of refinance is a sale and leaseback agreement, which involves a finance company 'buying' an asset from you, and then leasing it back to you under a financing agreement. Repayments are made, based on the value of the asset, and at the end of the term ownership reverts back to you. In some cases, assets you own under existing finance deals can be refinanced in this manner, making it a highly accessible method of releasing cash. The core benefits are thus:

- Flexible method of unlocking value of existing assets, with most types of plant, machinery or equipment being eligible for refinancing regardless of the size or type of business (sole trader or limited company, for example)
- Asset ownership reverts to you at the end of the term

Thankfully for businesses, asset finance is a fairly dynamic space with many providers, including some of the larger banking institutions. Specialist organisations also exist that finance specific forms of assets, such as plant, machinery or fleets of vehicles, and this proliferation means that you can often shop around to secure the best deal.

How can your accountant help?

Your accountant can be a useful ally in helping you with your asset purchases, particularly in the following areas:

- **Discussing your needs and helping you to formulate an asset investment strategy** – identifying specific needs are important to ensure you don't expend valuable cash or commit to long-term repayments unnecessarily
- **Preparing revenue forecasts or other financial reports** – many finance houses will require detailed financial information as part of any financing agreement
- **Undertaking investment appraisal or feasibility studies** – such reports can help you to ascertain the overall economic benefit of acquiring new assets. This may prove particularly useful for large, expensive assets or those that are linked with a new business direction or opportunity
- **Offer advice on ring-fencing to protect valuable assets** – methods exist to protect assets from claims or liabilities. Such methods may be fairly simple, or involve larger restructuring
- **Advising on tax implications associated with assets** – it is important to factor in any potential tax issues associated with acquiring assets

Ring-fencing

> "Everyone is a genius. But if you judge a fish by its ability to climb a tree, it will spend its whole life believing it is stupid."
>
> — *Einstein*

If you run your business through a limited company or LLP then you're already benefiting from ring-fencing, since your exposure to any personal liabilities (unless you have personal guarantees in place, or have acted unlawfully) is limited. Ring-fencing is therefore protecting those things that have value, such as assets, from any claims or liabilities.

For most businesses, or at least during the early part of a business's lifetime, this level of ring-fencing is probably sufficient. However, as your business grows, you become more profitable, more valuable; you might be increasing your workforce, diversifying into new, larger projects and increasing your investment in assets. This growth creates higher risk, with the business having more to lose, so you may start thinking about ring-fencing.

The most effective ring-fencing can be achieved by restructuring your business. Even the most successful businesses started out as a single company; they may be large groups of companies now but at one point they were probably a single entity. As needs change, it may be appropriate to consider the benefits of operating within a group structure:

Reasons for considering a group structure

- **To ring-fence valuable assets** in order to protect them against claims if the trading company is subject to litigation for whatever reason. In most cases, the assets that are usually ring-fenced are property based, such as the buildings from which the business operates.

    If these assets are left in the trading company, they are available to satisfy any claims made against the company, and therefore it makes sense to consider holding them separately. However, these assets will need to be held either **above** the trading company, i.e. in a holding company or another subsidiary of that holding company, or **outside** of the trading company, for example by one or more shareholders. Assets held in subsidiaries of the trading company are not ring-fenced.

- **For organisational reasons** – splitting different areas of your business operations into separate companies may be necessary as it grows and becomes exposed to differing risks. This helps spread risk, and limit contagion amongst different areas of your business.

- **Planning ahead for a potential sale of your business** – if you are planning on selling your business, you may not wish to sell the entire business or you may be able to maximise the sale value by selling parts at different times. In general, it is preferable to sell the shares of a limited company rather than its assets.

If you're thinking of ring-fencing then chances are your business is probably growing fast and possesses significant value – this highlights one of the issues with restructuring, which is a matter of timing and working out when is best to act. If you react too slowly or leave a ring-fencing restructure to a later stage, then things may become more complex and expensive.

Restructuring can be inherently complicated, and due to the uniqueness of individual businesses there is no one-size-fits-all solution – here, at least, we can only talk in general terms, so let's take a brief look at what you can expect to be involved within a simple holding company ring-fencing exercise…

Firstly, if you do decide to create a holding company structure, you need to consider which, if any, parts of the trading company should be transferred up to the new holding company to enable them to be protected.

The steps to achieve this are fairly simple, but need to be carried out properly otherwise there's a risk of two major problems. Firstly, in the event of a subsequent sale of the business, the deal may fall through if the purchaser cannot identify the ownership and history. Secondly, and perhaps more seriously, if there was a claim against the business the provision of the Insolvency Act may result in the assets transferred to the holding company being reclaimed to settle any liabilities; furthermore, these particular provisions are not time limited, so could be used many years after the transfer occurred.

Any assets transferred up to the new holding company must be transferred at **true market value**, as at the time of transfer; transfers at less will mean that the transaction is challengeable, and could result in the directors attracting personal liability for breach of the statutory duties that they owe to the company. Another proviso is that leaving few assets in a trading company may have a detrimental effect on its credit rating; this may have a knock-on effect when it comes to securing contracts.

Taking these factors into account, a summary of the steps needed is shown below in the order they need to be actioned.

- Obtain or incorporate a new company to become the new holding company.
- An appropriate professional should carry out a valuation of the existing company for the purpose of the share for share swap which puts the new holding company in place.
- Your accountant makes an application to HMRC for tax clearance for the share for share swap.
- Prepare a share swap agreement recording the share swap and supporting documentation, such as board resolutions and stock transfer forms.
- Consider whether there is any stamp duty payable on the share transfer. It should be possible to take advantage of one of the statutory reliefs, but the stock transfer forms on the share swap will need formal adjudication.
- If there are to be additional subsidiary companies of the new holding company, they should be formed now and adopt consistent Articles.

- If there are assets to be transferred from the existing company, whether to the new holding company or another subsidiary of that holding company, a short form asset sale agreement will be needed to record the sale and the market price. Often the sale price will be left outstanding on loan, and repaid out of dividends paid as the business develops – note the importance of market value in any sales agreement.
- Formalise the basis on which the original company uses the assets which it has transferred, such as a lease in the case of property.

We have seen the benefits of ring-fencing many times over the years, both clients that have learned the hard way, having elected not to invest in restructuring, and also those whose ring-fencing strategies have paid off.

CASE STUDY – Creating a holding company to protect assets

Following our advice, a client had all their equipment, cash and assets in a holding company, whilst the subsidiary trading company entered into a lucrative contract to construct an out-of-town DIY store. The main contractor, a major UK DIY chain, had their shares suspended when the Serious Fraud Office (SFO) were called in. At the time, the client had completed 50% of the £3 million works but had no money coming in from the main contractor. They also owed £1.2 million to subcontractors. **By ring-fencing, the client would have been able to liquidate the trading subsidiary – by no means an easy way out – but at least they would not have lost the equipment, cash or assets of the holding company.**

Pensions

> "Cessation of work is not accompanied by a cessation in expenses."
> — *Cato, Roman politician, first century BC*

We have always been passionate about planning for the future, whether it's retirement or estate planning, pensions, investments or just restructuring to hedge against the potential unknowns. For business owners, forward thinking is key; living day-to-day is just not a viable option.

Over our years in practice we have always strived to guide and empower our clients to effectively plan for the future. Understanding a client's needs, their business and aspirations is all necessary for forward planning. This separates a good accountant from a great accountant – actively taking an interest in the goals and desires of clients, and adding real value to their lives, both now and in the future. In the modern age, it is simply not enough to just address only the compliance side of preparing accounts and tax returns. One could even say offering only reactive advice is a dereliction of duty – **accountants must be proactive**!

For most people, planning for the future will involve pensions. Everyone knows about them, but do they understand them? Over recent times the pension landscape has changed dramatically, and our firm has invested considerably into demystifying the varying complexities, to break the magician's code.

Pension options for small business owners

For directors and small business owners, there are two primary options for pensions: a self-invested pension plan (SIPP) or a small self-administered scheme (SSAS). Much is known about SIPPs, and the relative merits of such pension schemes has seen almost £100 billion being invested in them. The SSAS, on the other hand, is less well known, yet offers – in our opinion, having examined the inherent complexities – a much better and more flexible option for small business owners, not least because they can invest in commercial property and make loans, up to a certain percentage of the net asset value of the scheme, back to the sponsoring employer.

Central features of SIPPs and SSASs

Both SIPPs and SSASs allow individuals, directors or business owners to contribute funds into a pension and to benefit from generous tax reliefs. Generally, contributions are capped at £40,000 per annum (tax year 2016/17) but are made net of 20% tax, meaning that the government tops up the contribution to the pension scheme; so if you made a contribution of £800, the pension scheme would receive £1,000. There is also a limit to the value of a pension fund, called the lifetime allowance, after which certain tax charges may arise. The current limit is £1 million.

The table below shows the tax benefits of personal contributions (as opposed to employer contributions) into a SIPP or SSAS:

Amount you pay (80%)	Government adds (20%)	Total invested in your SIPP	Higher rate tax payers can claim back a further	Effective cost for higher rate tax payers as little as
£800	£200	£1,000	£200	£600
£2,880*	£720	£3,600	£720	£2,160
£8,000	£2,000	£10,000	£2,000	£6,000
£16,000	£4,000	£20,000	£4,000	£12,000
£32,000	£8,000	£40,000	£8,000	£24,000

*maximum contribution for non-earners. You can contribute the equivalent of 100% of your earnings up to a maximum of £40,000. It is important to note that earnings in this context is restricted to employment income (salary and taxable benefits) or to self-employed income, so if you receive additional forms of income, such as dividends, interest or rent, then this would not be counted towards your maximum pension contribution. This annual pension contribution allowance is tapered for high income individuals. For every £2 of 'adjusted income' above £150,000, the annual allowance is reduced by £1. The maximum reduction is £30,000, meaning that someone with adjusted income of over £210,000 has an annual allowance of £10,000.

We won't go too much into the details of the UK pension system, but rather look at some of the key differences between SIPPs and SSASs:

- **Ownership** – the first difference is that anyone can set up a SIPP whether it's an individual, a business owner or a company but not everyone can set up a SSAS. A SSAS can only be set up in conjunction with the employer company of the founder member, and a limited number of twelve people can join the scheme, including the founder. Other members will typically be company directors or employees and their family members.
- **Ability** to advance a loan is a distinguishing factor between a SSAS and SIPP. Members of the SSAS can lend back up to 50% of the money in their pension back to the company, as long as it is secured. The security can be a business premises, a personal asset or another company. Any money loaned is not an interest-free loan, it must be paid back by the company with a reasonable rate of interest within HMRC guidelines.
- **Investment control** – a SSAS has greater freedom in the choice of investment it makes since the decisions are not made by a third party (such as the financial institution acting as the administrator for a SIPP) that may be more risk averse: they are set up by your company, so it is YOUR pension scheme. Additionally, a SSAS can invest up to 5% of its value in the shares of the sponsoring company (or in other unquoted shares) and if the business comprises more than one company, shares can be bought in multiple companies as long as the total invested is no more than 20% of the fund. This is another way for money to be loaned to the business from the pension to the benefit of the company.
- **Costs** – a SSAS is generally considered to be more expensive to operate than a SIPP, but this is pure perception and will completely depend on circumstances.

Small self-administered schemes (SSAS)

Much has been written about SIPPs, but less so about SSASs. Because of this, it's worth taking a closer look at SSASs.

A SSAS is governed by a Trust Deed and a set of rules, is a separate legal entity from the sponsoring company and is run by its trustees. Company contributions can be variable, depending on profitability, and no contractual obligation is in place to pay any specific contribution.

The scheme can make a wide range of investments including:

- Unlisted shares
- UK quoted stocks, shares, gilts and debentures
- Shares quoted on the Alternative Investment Market (AIM)
- Warrants, futures and options
- Permanent interest bearing shares (PIBS)
- Stocks and shares traded on a recognised overseas stock exchange
- Authorised unit trusts, investment trusts and Open-Ended Investment Companies (OEICs)
- Insurance company funds
- Deposit accounts
- Commercial property and land
- Hedge funds

Certain other investments could result in a tax charge, for example:

- Most notably, residential property and associated land
- Loans to connected parties such as scheme members, their relatives and partnerships in which they are partners

Headline tax and other benefits include:

- Employer contributions are allowable as an expense against corporation tax
- Investments accumulate free of income tax and CGT
- A percentage of the fund can be paid out as a tax free lump sum on retirement, or potentially all of the fund on death
- Fees can be paid by the sponsoring company, and are tax deductible
- No insurance nor third party administration required

The scheme can invest tax efficiently in commercial land and property, including purchasing from and/or leasing back to the company. This is highly desirable since the purchasing from the company can ensure the business can raise funds, but the trustees retain control. Additionally, property held by the scheme is protected from creditors of the company, and any rental income or capital gains are free of tax. The maximum borrowing that can be utilised by the SSAS is 50% of the current scheme value, although joint purchase (for example, with the company) can also be considered.

For us, the choice is clear: **SSASs represent a really attractive option for small business owners for numerous reasons**, and we actively recommend these to our clients. Whilst setting up and running your own pension scheme might seem daunting, in reality and with the right advice and support, it needn't be so.

Here's our step by step guide on how to easily set up and run a SSAS.

1. **Prepare the SSAS by drafting a pension scheme trust deed**. This formally establishes the pension scheme.
2. **The SSAS can have one trustee**, but to avoid any issues resulting if the sole trustee dies, **it's recommended to have two trustees** – usually the business owner and spouse.

3. **Appoint a scheme administrator.** The administrator registers the SSAS with HMRC and makes the relevant statutory returns. They will first themselves need to be registered with HMRC as an administrator: https://www.gov.uk/guidance/pension-administrators-register-as-an-administrator.

4. **Register the pension scheme with HMRC.** This is a simple online process by visiting https://www.gov.uk/guidance/pension-administrators-register-a-scheme. HMRC will issue a certificate, and it's best to use a home address for confidentiality purposes.

5. **Setting up a bank account.** Once you have received a certificate from HMRC, you can open up a bank account. The bank will also want to see the pension scheme trust deed. You can set up the usual banking preferences – signatories, internet banking, authorisation levels and CHAPS limits.

6. **All contributions from the sponsoring employers can now be paid in gross.**

7. **If you have an existing SIPP, then contact the provider to transfer the funds into the new SSAS.** They will need the SSAS reference number, and, if the existing SIPP is cash, it can just be transferred into the new SSAS bank account.

8. **If the existing SIPP holds assets**, i.e. investments in shares or unit trusts, then an **'in specie' transfer is required**, reregistering these assets under the SSAS.

9. **Once the SSAS has funds, you can make investments.** Be very careful about what investments you make, as the penalties for breaching rules are severe.

10. **Prepare annual accounts.** There is a requirement to prepare yearly accounts, and if 5th April is chosen as the year end, then no audit is required. The format of the accounts is not important, as they are not required to be

submitted anywhere. A convenient format for the accounts can be discussed with your accountant.

11. **File an online return**. In theory, the online return is only required if HMRC issues a notice. In practice, however, one is required each year. The deadline is 31st January, much the same as self-assessment tax returns. Penalties exist for late filing, and it must be submitted electronically.

12. **If a tax refund is required, then an SA970 is submitted**. This is usually submitted if certain investments are paid net of tax, so any tax deducted can be reclaimed. Even if this reclaim is only required for one year, then HMRC will usually request or issue a notice to submit an SA970 for the next few years, even if the return will be nil. HMRC will issue a 10-digit self-assessment number.

13. **The Pension Regulator (TPR)**. If there is more than one member of the SSAS, then the scheme will need to be registered with TPR. If registration is required, an annual fee of £35 per member is due.

14. **New members.**
    - You can bring in new members but TPR must be notified
    - If a new member is added, be very careful with the records of the pension scheme because you must be able to split the fund and show contributions; you can use designated funds, or just split funds on a sensible and reasonable basis
    - Be careful about costs and how to split these.

15. **Fixed protection.** If the fund exceeds the new limit of £1 million, then consider taking fixed protection.

16. **Fees.** The pension scheme fees can be paid by the sponsoring employer, who can claim tax relief and VAT relief.

17. **On retirement.**
    - At age 55 or over you can retire.
    - You are entitled to take out 25% of the value of the scheme tax free. There are lots of options about when and how to do

this, depending on your age and other factors which would best be discussed with your accountant or financial advisor.
- You can purchase an annuity for all or part, but if you secure an annual pension of at least £20,000, which at the current rate at 55 years old costs about £430,000, then you can draw out all the income produced as a 'salary' or pension drawing.
- Any pension drawn is run through a pension PAYE scheme, where income tax is deducted but National Insurance is not applicable.
- If a pension has started to be drawn, the whole of the fund has a special status and cannot be transferred tax free on death. However, if there has been careful planning and appropriately nominated beneficiaries, the scheme can continue to pay out a pension, taxed via PAYE, to the widow or other beneficiaries.
- It's possible to divide the SSAS into two funds, use one part for an annuity, and keep the other part in the SSAS growing tax free. If you have not yet drawn any of the second fund and you die before the age of 75, this can be transferred out tax free on death to your spouse or other beneficiaries.

18. **Loans received.** The pension scheme can borrow up to 50% of its value, but certain HMRC guidelines apply regarding the interest rate charged and repayment terms if the loan is from a connected party. Current guidelines are 1% over base rate.

19. **Commercial property.** The scheme can purchase commercial property, and the scheme can be VAT registered to deal with any VAT on commercial properties, etc.
    Care needs to be taken with property, especially anything residential or that has the potential to become residential, as the penalties for this breach of scheme rules is severe.

We are strong advocates of SSASs; they allow you take control of your investments, have flexibility in the area of commercial property transactions or the ability to make loans to the employer, and have the potential to generate a greater return than SIPPs, which tend to be managed by more conservative administrators. But, whichever you choose, a pension plan should form one part of your overall retirement strategy. A good accountant will be able to help develop a successful retirement plan, the main components being to:

- **Plan well ahead** – it is never too early to start planning for your retirement. The earlier you start the greater your chance of reaching your goal.
- **Be flexible and balanced** – work toward an appropriate balance between high and low risk exposure, and keep flexible options open across a diverse range of instruments such as pensions, savings, investments and insurance.
- **Work with professionals** – the decisions you make now will affect your future. Your accountant can assist with finding a good Independent Financial Advisor (IFA).

As with most complex financial issues, it is always recommended to seek professional advice, and make informed decisions based on your own specific circumstances.

Jeffrey Lermer and Karen Wyrwas

Partnership and shareholder disputes

> "Measure your success by how well you obtain your goals – not how well you get along with your partner."
>
> — *Anon*

Partnerships are popular ways of running businesses, and this can be a small, loose association between two partners who are registered as such with HMRC, or a more formal legal structure such as an LLP. They allow groups of people to come together for the purposes of running a business, often with skills that complement or form some natural synergy with other partners. However, it's a fact of life that people do not get on all of the time, drift apart or want to go their own separate ways to pursue other business opportunities. And the construction industry, with its inherent challenges and pressures, can be a difficult place to work and maintain cordial relations – disputes within this industry are commonplace.

Partnership agreements

If you work in partnership, or are perhaps thinking of setting one up, then one thing that shouldn't be overlooked is having a formal written partnership agreement in place. It's true that most partnerships function perfectly well with no agreements in place, and the very nature of entering into a business partnership with other parties would imply that some degree of mutual trust in the integrity and capabilities of the respective individuals exists. However, what happens if a partner dies, becomes bankrupt, distances themselves from the business and responsibilities, acts dishonestly, or uses the partnership assets to pursue separate business activities?

Whatever the underlying reasons, when it becomes apparent that the continuation of a partnership business is no longer a viable option, it is possible to dissolve it without resorting to court action, provided the partners involved express some willingness to co-operate with each other in pursuit of an orderly dissolution or buyout. Often, this is easier said than done.

If the business partners have had the foresight to enter into a partnership agreement then this will normally make clear provisions for the expulsion of a partner in certain circumstances, and for a structured and agreeable dissolution if this should become necessary.

However, where there is no partnership agreement in place, or where the formal agreement does not make adequate provision for the dissolution or expulsion of a partner, then court action may prove unavoidable. The process of going through the courts is expensive and time-consuming, and – regardless of the outcome – it may have serious consequences for the survival of the business itself. It is really to be used only as a procedure of last resort where other avenues, such as mediation or some form of dispute resolution, have been exhausted.

The key, therefore, is to ensure that prior to entering into a partnership you **have a binding partnership agreement in place**, that is sufficiently explicit in its provisions to cover all reasonable eventualities. If you do not have such an agreement, then the best course of action would be to get one drawn up as soon as possible – a specialist accountant who is familiar with the intricacies of the construction sector would be the first place to look for commercial guidance, and then work with a lawyer to put it into legalese. Going straight to a lawyer, in our experience, can result in considerably higher costs.

Dissolution through the courts

If it is necessary to do so, a court may grant a decree of dissolution when any partner, other than the one pursuing the dissolution:

- Is suffering from a permanent incapacity
- Has conducted himself in a way that is detrimental to the business or is calculated to prejudicially affect the continuance of the business
- Is in breach of the partnership agreement or has conducted himself in such a way that it is not reasonably practicable for the other partner to carry on the partnership business with him

A court may also grant a decree of dissolution under the following circumstances:

- It is just and equitable to do so – this covers a wide range of situations
- Where the partnership can only trade at a loss

What is the effect of dissolution?

In the event of a court-imposed dissolution of a partnership, the business continues but only insofar as is necessary to wind the business up. This means to discharge any outstanding liabilities and to distribute the surplus assets and cash between the partners.

In a situation where there is an outgoing partner and the business is to continue, using the accumulated capital and assets of the partnership and without any final settlement of accounts, then the outgoing partner is entitled to such a share of ongoing profits made since dissolution as the court attribute to the use of partnership assets, or to award interest payable at the rate of 5% per year on the amount of his share of the partnership assets.

Otherwise where the only outcome is dissolution, final settlement of accounts is imperative – this involves trading only to complete ongoing business transactions before winding the business up. Each of the partners would then be entitled to a share of the final net assets of the business.

Alternatives

Obviously court action to dissolve a partnership is expensive, time-consuming and can descend quite rapidly into animosity. Other options are available, including formal dispute resolution channels or mediation. These routes may lead the partnership to some of the following alternatives:

A partner, or any number of partners, may give **notice to dissolve** a partnership and for it to carry on in business for only as long as it is necessary to wind the business up. This notice must be given with sufficient time to enable, where applicable, any ongoing business matters to be transferred to a new entity. If the business is to be dissolved then provision will need to be made for any dissolution costs that may arise, such as outstanding tax liabilities, surrender of leased premises, equipment leasing agreements, and so on.

Another option is for one or more partners to '**buy out**' the partnership interest of the remaining partners. In the absence of any stipulated buyout price or settlement within the terms of a partnership agreement, then the buyout price would normally be equivalent to the amount to which a leaving partner would be entitled upon dissolution – i.e. once the final settlement of accounts has been completed and the residual net asset value has been apportioned to each partner, taking into account any adjustments that may be appropriate. Any buyout must also settle other matters between the parties involved; outgoing partners may wish to be indemnified against future liabilities, such as financing guarantees, leasing obligations or other contractual liabilities. The remaining partner may also insist on reciprocal covenants which restrict the outgoing partner from engaging in business activities that may impact the business and therefore exert a retrospective adjustment on the fair value of the buyout.

A final point to note is that the partnership most likely employs a number of staff, and if it is to continue trading under a new business entity then employees would simply transfer to the new business under a Transfer of Undertakings (TUPE) procedure, meaning that employees' rights, for example holiday entitlement, etc. are protected. However, if the partnership dissolves with no similar business to replace it, then the employees will be redundant and may be entitled to a redundancy payment from the partnership, which will need to be settled before the final distribution of net assets is carried out.

It is clear that **it's in the interests of all parties within a partnership to establish some formal written partnership agreement** to help protect against the uncertainty and expense that may arise as a result of any dispute or dissolution proceedings. Similarly, **for limited companies, establishing a shareholder's agreement is equally important** since many of the matters raised also hold true.

The points made in this chapter are for illustrative purposes only; there's no magic formula for resolving disputes or constructing partnership or shareholder agreements. Individual situations and circumstances will determine the sort of agreement and resolution mechanisms that you may require. **Professional advice is always recommended.**

Contractor disputes

> "When you're at the edge of a cliff, progress is a step backwards."
> — *A wise lemming*

It's probably fair to say that construction contracts cannot cater for every eventuality, and because of this, whenever problems arise, either party may have a vested interest in gaining as much as they can from the other. Equally, in the event of a dispute, contractors or subcontractors may each have a different perception of the facts, or have unrealistic expectations which can affect their ability to reach some form of common agreement or compromise. Alternatively, one of the contracted parties may simply deny responsibility in an attempt to avoid any liability. The fact is that contractor disputes are an unfortunate, and not uncommon, occurrence in the construction industry.

A recent survey of the UK construction industry, carried out by RIBA Enterprises, revealed an increasing trend of disputes across the sector*. From a sample of 1,000 contractors, subcontractors and consultants, 30% had been involved in one or more disputes over the preceding year, with 7% reporting they had been involved in three or more disputes. The overall perception amongst those businesses surveyed was that the financial pressures of the industry, a consequence of low margins, lack of access to financing and cash intensive operational costs, were creating an adversarial environment between contractors and other parties. Against this backdrop, it is worth trying to understand some of the common causes of contractor dispute, so you can reduce the risks for your own construction business.

Common causes of construction disputes

Construction is a unique and complex process which can give rise to some unusual and unique disputes.

* National Construction Contracts and Law Survey 2013 (https://www.thenbs.com/about-nbs/news/nbs-survey-reveals-an-increase-in-construction-industry-disputes)

Acceleration

It is not uncommon for contractors to insist upon acceleration of a construction project. A common example might be a commercial property project or fit-out, and the need to meet specific deadlines for opening or tenant occupation. In such cases, the construction costs associated with accelerating the work may be less than the commercial risk of failing to meet key deadlines. If the exact circumstances surrounding construction acceleration are not properly analysed and accounted for, then this may lead to a dispute if the subcontractor or contractor has incurred additional costs in carrying out the accelerative measures only to find that the owner of the project refuses to pay.

Delays

Disputes frequently arise in respect of delays and who should bear responsibility for them. Most construction contracts make provision for extending the time for completion, and the primary reason for this is so that the owner of the contract can keep alive any rights to delay damages recoverable from a contractor or subcontractor.

Design errors

Errors in design, such as architectural plans, installation instructions or similar, can lead to delays and additional costs that have the potential to become the subject of disputes. Sometimes those responsible for the design errors may attempt to absolve themselves of any responsibility, leaving the contractors drawn into trying to solve any deficiencies to avoid delays and meet construction deadlines. This could lead to subsequent design failures and exposure to risk.

Co-ordination problems

In more complex construction projects, particularly those that involve specialist trades such as installation work – plumbing, electrical or mechanical, etc. – the co-ordination amongst subcontractors is key. Yet conflict often arises because the work is not properly co-ordinated, and this inevitably leads to delays which are costly and time-consuming to resolve, with each party blaming the other for the problems that have arisen.

Quality and workmanship

In traditional construction contracts, disputes often arise as to whether or not the completed work is in accordance with the specifications. The specification may be vague on the subject of the dispute, and each party to the contract may have a different view on whether the quality and workmanship is acceptable. In design and build contracts, perhaps the greatest deficiency is in the contract documentation, particularly the project owners' requirements. This inadequacy inevitably leads to claims by the contractor for additional costs which, if not resolved, can lead to expensive disputes.

Site conditions

If the contract inadequately describes which party is to take the risk for the site conditions, disputes are inevitable when adverse site or ground conditions impede the progress of work or require more expensive engineering solutions.

Tender

The time allowed to scrutinise the tender documents, prepare an outline programme and methodology, carry out a risk assessment, calculate the price, and conclude the whole process with a commercial review is often impossibly short. Mistakes in this process may have an adverse effect on the successful commercial outcome of the project. A culture may be engendered of pursuing every claim that has a prospect of redressing any ultimate financial shortfall. This approach does nothing to foster close and co-operative working relationships between the owner and the contractor during the progress of the work, and inevitably leads to disputes.

Variations

Variations are a prime cause of construction disputes, particularly where there are a substantial number, or the variations impact on partially completed work or are issued as work is nearing completion. The nature and number of variations can transform a relatively straightforward project into one of unmanageable complexity.

These are just some of the more common causes of dispute within the construction industry. It can often appear that if you put one contractor in a room on his own he will end up in dispute! Thankfully, there is a fairly strong dispute resolution framework in the UK that can help antagonising parties resolve their differences. Sensible construction contracts will often specify how dispute resolution will be applied in the event of a dispute.

Dispute resolution

There are a number of dispute resolution techniques, the basic principles of which are summarised below.

- **Negotiation:** The process whereby the parties work out between them how to resolve any issues that have arisen. Power to settle the dispute rests with the parties.

- **Mediation and conciliation:** The parties agree on an independent, third party neutral system to facilitate discussions between them, with the goal of reaching a settlement. The power to settle remains with the parties, but the process is led by the mediator.
- **Expert determination:** The parties agree by a contract that a third party will make a binding decision on them. The terms are therefore governed by the contract. In most cases the decision of an expert will be final, and it will not be possible to appeal that decision. This means that the decision of an expert finally determines the dispute without further recourse.
- **Arbitration:** For arbitration to apply, the contract between the parties must contain a written agreement to arbitrate. Where it applies, the parties might choose to refer to or incorporate an arbitration procedure, such as the Construction Industry Model Arbitration Rules. Alternatively, the arbitration can simply be covered by the applicable legislation, such as the Arbitration Act 1996.
- **Litigation:** The courts have inherent jurisdiction to hear a dispute in respect of just about anything. In the absence of any other dispute resolution procedure, the parties will at least have a right to refer their matter to an appropriate court. The procedure is governed by the Civil Procedure Rules, and the nature, complexity and value of the dispute will determine which court will hear a particular dispute. Courts have the widest jurisdiction, and in addition to determining disputes and declarations, they can also summon witnesses and involve third parties in the dispute as necessary. In some circumstances a clear debt may be more economically and easily obtained by serving a Statutory Demand or a Winding Up Petition rather than commencing an action in the court.

- **Dispute boards:** Dispute boards are an effective mechanism for dispute avoidance, resolution and management of contractual disputes on medium to large scale projects. Dispute boards usually exist throughout the duration of a contract and can be referred to at any time by any one of the parties to make a recommendation or determination of the dispute referred. They are commonly made up of professionals, who possess relevant qualifications and associations within the construction industry. A dispute board involved with the project or venture from inception through to completion has 'hands on' knowledge of every aspect of the project, it therefore knows the parties, goals and objectives, and is able to act very quickly, either to prevent a dispute from arising or to give a timely decision, in some cases as soon as 30 days after the formal request.

Our Guest Chapter 17 will look at contract issues in more depth from a legal perspective.

Guest chapter: Contracts

> "A verbal contract isn't worth the paper it is written on."
> — *Samuel Goldwyn*

This chapter is written by Laurence Cobb, who is a Partner at Taylor Wessing LLP, a forward-thinking and dynamic international law firm with offices in over 30 major cities across the globe.

We looked briefly at disputes in the previous chapter, and this chapter provides a more comprehensive overview of common issues arising out of building projects of all shapes and sizes with reference to which terms of dealing affect the parties to such a transaction. There are many excellent detailed text books, case law, statutes and articles on what is in its entirety a wide and complex area of the law, and if the reader identifies or recognises issues relevant to him or her, then reference to such works and/or seeking independent legal advice is recommended.

With the above in mind, let us start our whistle-stop journey through some common contractual and legal issues relevant to the construction world.

The contract

A building contract, whether for a small house extension or a major infrastructure project, is where one party, in return for something of value, agrees to carry out construction or engineering work for another party. This may include design and/or project management services, or those services may be carried out by others such as an architect by way of a separate agreement for such services and, as we will see later, the extent of what is being provided is often a key issue between the parties.

A contract is best recorded in writing, but can be oral or a mixture of both, but if elements are oral, then there may be arguments and differing evidence as to what terms have been agreed.

Has the contract been formed?

The clearest evidence of formation of a contract is when a document is actually signed. If a contract, often on an industry standard form, is signed it may be signed by hand or executed as a deed. This is relevant to the time that liability will remain in place between the parties and should be carefully checked as it can make a significant difference to the risk profile of the project. Often contractors obtain projects based on a tender which makes reference to contract documents. If subsequently the contract is never executed, then it is more than likely that the terms set out in the tender document will be seen as those applying to the parties. It may also be the case that the contract is administered as if those particular terms applied, which will go towards demonstrating the agreed relationship.

It is important to be careful to read all contractual documents. Building contracts are often formed of a number of parts such as, in the case of a design and build contract, employer's requirements and contractor's proposals. It is important to make sure that any contract refers to all the correct documents as there are often disputes in relation to clashes between documents in the same suite as to which takes precedence.

You may also find, particularly in relation to contracts for the supply of materials only, that each party endeavours to apply their own terms and conditions to the project. If you want your terms to apply it is important that you have the last communication of importance in that regard so that it is your terms that apply to the contract, although each set of circumstances is dependent upon its own facts.

Letters of intent

Sometimes, when the parties consider they are not quite ready to enter into a detailed contract but want the work to start, a letter of intent is issued to enable the project to get under way. Such letters often have a cap as to time and/or maximum spend before they expire. They are prone to lead to disputes due to their wording being unclear or the parties continuing to operate on the letter of intent way beyond the financial cap as they are unable to agree the full terms of the contract. If you are working with a letter of intent make yourself aware of its scope and take care regarding what it requires you to do and your entitlement to be paid for such works, before a building contract is agreed and signed to replace it.

Standard forms of contract

Most readers will be familiar with the various suites of standard forms of contract such as the JCT family of contracts and more recently the NEC family of contracts. They do tend to come in all shapes and sizes appropriate to the scale and nature of the job but do make sure that the standard form is one you are familiar with and, in particular, be aware of the extent of any design responsibilities (if any) and other requirements that are placed upon you. If, as sometimes happens, there is simply a reference to a particular published standard form contract as being applicable without further information it is quite likely that that form of contract will apply regardless of that fact so you need to know what is in it.

Also, be aware of the fact that many of the standard form contracts are heavily amended and it is important to check those amendments so that you understand what has changed from the standard position.

Statutory terms

In addition to those terms agreed between the parties by way of commercial bargain there is some legislation that will affect the parties' rights and position. These include the Unfair Contract Terms Act 1977, the Housing Grants, Construction and Regeneration Act 1996 and the Defective Premises Act 1979, as well as various regulations in areas such as health and safety, most notably the Construction (Design and Management) Regulations 2015. Ignorance of this legislation is unlikely to be a defence so it is important that you are aware of such responsibilities, particularly if you are operating in the residential market.

Contractual matrix/insurance

It is vitally important as a contractor that you have the insurances required under the contract, particularly public liability insurance and contractor's all risks insurance for the works, but also in the case of design, professional indemnity insurance. Equally important is that the insurance needs to be at an appropriate level to cover the exposure and risk. In some cases, these policies will be joint as between the employer and the contractor.

Regarding the contractual matrix, the area of construction is probably one of the most complex in relation to the number of parties that are involved in a project both from the point of view of ensuring that the project is built but also in relation to consultancy services such as project management, design, quantity surveying and engineering. It is important that you are clear as to where your responsibilities begin and end and also insofar as you have subcontracted some of your responsibilities to others that the agreements are what is known as 'back to back' i.e. that you have passed on any liability in its entirety to the party to whom you have delegated the task.

Warranties/bonds/guarantees

As well as direct contracts between the parties, most of you will be familiar with the fact that requirements are often placed upon parties to provide warranties to third parties such as funders or landlords and for subcontractors to provide warranties to the ultimate employer.

In addition, and by way of security, there are sometimes requirements for parent company guarantees and in some cases performance bonds to be provided by the contractor to give security against failures. These are often in addition to any retentions held under the contract up to the end of the project and the making good of defects. This particular topic could form a significant textbook in itself, but for the purposes of this chapter you should simply be aware of those requirements and seek further advice regarding the effect of such documents.

Common issues during the project

Assuming that a recognisable form of contract has been agreed, we then move into the commencement of the project. Whilst issues potentially arising under a contract can be many and varied, and there is no substitute for an ongoing dialogue between the parties to try and resolve issues, there are nonetheless some common themes that emerge where difficulties may arise.

- **Valuations/payment**

    The contract should set out the basis upon which payment is to be made and what is included within that payment. There is often a payment certifying process by a third party such as an architect or contract administrator and periods of time are set down for interim payments on a regular basis throughout the project, depending on its length, and culminating in the practical completion of the project. An element of the retention deducted as a matter of course throughout the project is usually released at practical completion pending resolution of any outstanding defective items during a defects liability period. There are likely to be detailed valuation processes as to how items are valued and these should be followed. The real key in the process, particularly bearing in mind the Housing Grants, Construction and Regeneration Act 1996 and its associated Scheme for Construction Contracts, is to comply precisely with the timings for when applications for payment should be submitted and notices of payment, or 'pay less' notices, served. It is good idea at the outset of the contract to set up your own schedule setting out these dates clearly and communicating them between the parties to avoid uncertainties as to timing.

- **Notices**

    Where there is a requirement to serve a notice regarding payment or any other issue under the contract such as a variation, it is vital that you adhere to such processes and the timing required either in the contract or under statute. If you fail to do so in some cases this can be fatal to recovery, such as complying with the payment notice requirements or alternatively under some contracts giving notice of potential and/or actual delay. There are strict notice requirements regarding payment notices under the Housing Grants, Construction and Regeneration Act 1996 which may apply to your contract whether or not set out in writing, so make sure that you are aware of and follow them as failure to comply can be very costly.

- **Disruption/delay**

    It is important to bear in mind that in many contracts claims for additional time and claims for extra time-related money are covered under separate clauses and it is important to note and apply this distinction when making any applications.

    Having a clear contract programme at the outset of the project is key to being able to demonstrate such delays and indeed showing the critical path through the programme to get to completion.

    There are many delay experts who deal with programming who spend a lot of time, energy and effort reviewing the position regarding contract progress both from a project management point of view and, if things go awry, a claims management point of view. It is important that the provisions under the contract are followed regarding such claims and that excellent records are kept, as usually the party that keeps the best records is likely to be more successful in relation to any claims.

- **Suspension/termination**

    There are likely to be provisions in your contract as to when you are entitled to suspend or when you are entitled to terminate. These provisions apply to both parties and it is likely that there will be different rights depending on the reason for suspension or termination. Again, it is important to follow the notice provisions in the contract and be sure to be clear in any correspondence regarding any termination threats whether they are for non-payment or non-performance or other reasons. This particular area is prone to disputes and there are fairly significant consequences if processes are not followed. If a contract is silent as to termination provisions one has to refer to the common law to see if the breach of one party was so serious as to entitle the other party to terminate the contract. Again, in this particular area, be very careful as to your steps.

- **Defects**

    This is an obvious area for concern both during and after completion of a project. In some cases, defects will either prevent the project from being completed or, alternatively, if a defect comes to light after the project has been completed, cause much difficulty regarding where responsibility lies as to liability. Indeed, where defects materialise a significant time after project completion there can be further complication as to whether the party who was primarily responsible for such issues is still solvent. Early notification of defects is definitely for the best.

Methods of dispute resolution

There are a number of methods of dispute resolution. These are often set out in the contract. If the contract is completely silent as to the method of dispute resolution then, if it is a construction contract, it is likely that the routes available, putting to one side mediation/alternative dispute resolution which we will come to later, will be the routes of the courts and/or adjudication.

- **Adjudication**

    Providing that a construction contract is in existence, whether or not a provision is made permitting adjudication under the contract, under the Housing Grants, Construction and Regeneration Act 1996, adjudication will be available to either party once a dispute has crystallised. It is now very difficult to argue that adjudication is commenced prematurely once the parties have differences between them. Adjudication is an interim but binding dispute resolution process which is designed to take a period of 28 days. In practice, it often takes longer than that but it is a quick process for resolving disputes and is generally recognised because of its tight timeline to be one where it is impossible to go into everything in full detail. Some see this process as rough justice. Whilst it is undoubtedly a much faster process than others available, care needs to be taken as to whether it is the appropriate forum for resolving your particular dispute given that it is seen as better suited to payment disputes rather than for delay and extension of time claims. The advantages of taking the adjudication route are ones that you clearly need to weigh up, although it is more likely than not that it will be the first formal dispute resolution process of choice, and certainly to be considered if negotiations have failed.

- **Arbitration**

    As an alternative to court proceedings, many contracts provide (and they have to do so in order for this route to be available) for the parties to go to arbitration, which is a private dispute resolution process but equally as binding as a decision of the court. Whilst arbitration is much more common and accepted for international contracts, it has become much less common concerning domestic contracts with parties preferring to take the adjudication route or the court route. Please bear in mind that with standard form contracts there are various appendices that need to be completed in relation to whether arbitration will apply and they are one of the most commonly missed or wrongly completed sections of a building contract. Whatever route you decide to take regarding the opportunity for dispute resolution, please ensure that these sections are completed fully and consistently. The default position under many standard form contracts is that if the dispute forum provisions are not completed, then any dispute will be referred to court.

- **The courts**

    In the event that the court is stated to be the forum for dispute resolution in the contract, or the contract is silent on that issue, and subject to the availability of adjudication referred to above then the route for dispute resolution will be that of the courts. For disputes above a certain value these will be referred to the Technology and Construction Court, which is a court specialising in technology and construction disputes. The judges in this particular arena are highly familiar with the area of construction law and will take a proactive role in endeavouring to ensure that disputes are resolved expeditiously and fairly. There are important pre-action procedures that one needs to take before referring matters to the court. Again, when it comes to availability and choice of the appropriate forum to have your disputes resolved independent advice at the outset is strongly recommended.

Cost of disputes

If one goes down the arbitration or court route, then legal and some other related costs in relation to bringing such a dispute are potentially recoverable by a winning party against a losing party, although there are a number of factors which may affect that entitlement.

In the case of adjudication, the position is different and each party must bear their own costs. Regarding the costs of the tribunal, if a matter is referred to an arbitrator then the parties will have responsibility for the arbitrator's costs (which indeed is the case with the adjudicator's costs) subject to the tribunal's view as to who should be responsible for those costs.

Other methods of dispute resolution

On rare occasions one might come across an expert determination provision in a contract which requires matters to be referred to an expert. Please note that if that is the case, it can be that the expert's decision is final and binding and not capable of being challenged in any other forum such as the courts. In the light of this, one needs to be comfortable with that scenario both in relation to its application to issues under the contract and the appropriateness of the appointed expert.

There has been over recent years, in part due to cost pressures of disputes, the encouragement of the courts and a general shift in the commercial market for alternative dispute resolution, a trend which has seen mediation be much more commonplace in the construction sector. This is a non-binding, without prejudice process where the mediator assists in trying to facilitate the parties to reach a settlement without actually being involved in representing either of the parties or giving a decision as to which party has an entitlement. This is definitely a growth area for resolution of disputes and has its attractions as, if successful, it is a much cheaper route to dispute resolution than protracted litigation.

Other related dispute resolution issues

As mentioned earlier, the route to dispute resolution that a party can take will to a certain extent be dependent on what has been provided for in the contract. Whilst the option of adjudication under a construction contract is always likely to be on the menu, there may under the contract provisions be dispute escalation clauses which provide for certain processes to be followed before the matter becomes a full dispute, such as reference to board members of the parties to the contract and/or an independently appointed team by way of a dispute resolution board. It is important to note that if these processes are in the contract they should be adhered to or at least advice should be taken as to whether there are hoops that have to be gone through before some of the other dispute resolution processes can be exercised.

One other area which returns back to the issue of the complicated contractual matrix in construction projects is that it may well be that there are a number of parties that are potentially wholly or partly liable for the same or similar issues under the contract. It is important that if dispute resolution clauses are put into those contracts that they interlink so that it is possible to ensure that all potential defendants are in the same dispute. For example, if the building contract has an arbitration clause but the architect's appointment does not, there is a risk of two separate proceedings for the same dispute which cannot be brought together, an outcome which can be very costly and produce contradictory results in a worst case scenario.

Summary

This chapter is very much a whistle-stop tour through some of the major issues under construction contracts and is intended simply to provide some helpful hints as to issues to consider in the event that you are involved in the construction industry. There is no substitute if you have a particular issue to obtaining good advice.

Laurence Cobb, Taylor Wessing LLP

Laurence Cobb — Breaking Ground

Guest chapter: Insurance

> "It is hard to fail, but it is worse never to have tried to succeed."
> — T. Roosevelt

M&DH Insurance Services Ltd (est. 2002) is a specialist broker in the construction industry that is truly independent from insurance companies. This provides clients with confidence that their best intentions are at the heart of what M&DH offer. With exclusive schemes into the Lloyds market, further explained below, the sole aim is to find the correct policy for the business without having to worry about outsider influence. All of M&DH's commercial insurance consultants hold the certificate qualification in insurance, and their staff are specialists within their field, each being bound by the code of conduct outlined by the Chartered Insurance Institute. In short, the benefit of opting for an independent broker such as M&DH is that they are not bound to keep your policy with the same insurer due to vested interests. Should your holding insurer fail to be the most competitive at renewal, M&DH will place your policy elsewhere in order to meet your needs and requirements.

A brief history of the modern insurance system

Put simply, insurance is the transfer of an unknown risk or loss against a known amount. This known amount is called a 'premium'. During the seventeenth century, the concept of insurance was becoming an increasingly attractive alternative for shipping companies who had experienced the effects of a total loss at sea. The place where this exchange took place wouldn't be your first guess, the Bank of England for example; instead the meeting took place at Edward Lloyd's Coffee House in Tower Street where sailors, merchants and ship owners would meet to hear reliable shipping news. Some wealthier people were willing to cover the cost in the event of a ship being lost at sea and in return they would charge their premium. Gradually syndicates formed and collectively started to cover the risk and would share the premium between them. Each member would agree to cover a certain percentage and would receive that percentage in the premium paid. The Lloyds marketplace became the place to go if you wanted Marine Insurance and this grew into the Lloyds of London that we know today, currently situated in Lime Street in London.

Types of products

For companies that have employees, as defined in the policy wording, then **Employers Liability** insurance is required by law. Introduced through the Employers Liability (Compulsory Insurance) Act 1969, this provides indemnity for the company's legal liabilities for injury to employees consequent upon death or bodily injury arising out of the course of each person's employment. Cover can also extend to include legal costs and expenses incurred in defending prosecutions under Health and Safety legislation. The minimum level of cover required by law is £5,000,000. However, most insurers will offer £10,000,000 as a blanket start, as this is the only legally required insurance policy for most construction companies. This will be the only policy that will have a certificate as proof of cover.

Public liability insurance is not yet legally required, but is strongly recommended for all companies who work in the construction industry. Without this cover, the company themselves would have to cover the cost of any claim incurred. This provides indemnity for legal liability for injury to the public for loss of or damage to property not owned by you, or in your custody or control. Some tenders will only be considered if they hold a high enough level of insurance. Without this cover, the contractor themselves would be responsible to cover the cost of any damage or injury caused to third persons and third party property. Cover can start from £1,000,000 and can be increased to a desired sum through the use of excess layers. These are separate policies that will start once the primary layer (original insurers) limit has been reached. For example, a contractor may have £10,000,000 public liability insurance; however, the primary insurer will only offer to write £5,000,000 limit of indemnity for public liability. In this event, an excess layer of £5,000,000 will be required. This cover is usually based on each and every claim; so in this case they would have £10,000,000 to cover **each** claim experienced within one policy period.

Whilst talking about third party damage, **product liability** is closely linked and is very often included as a standard extension of cover. This provides indemnity for accidental bodily injury, accidental loss or damage to the property of third parties arising from defects in goods you manufacture, sell, supply, test, service or maintain. This works on the basis that if a product is supplied and it appears to be faulty at the point of installation then the first person to encounter a claim will be that person to supply the good. The level of cover usually matches the level of cover for the public liability and can be increased through the use of excess layers. This cover is usually in the aggregate which means there is a set amount to cover the combined cost of **all** claims within one policy period.

Contract works insurance will cover the work in progress on a construction site for a wide range of perils including, but not limited to, fire, flood and malicious damage. A good example is a contractor building an extension to an existing property; the contract works policy will provide cover for the new works as it is being erected along with the materials and fittings. There is the option for the contractor to self-insure and cover the cost of starting the works again as their client will not pay them twice for the same contract. Premiums are calculated based on the maximum contract value and will cover all insurable claims up to this limit. If Contractor A has one contract of £1,000,000 that will last the entirety of the policy period and will not be carrying out any further work then their maximum contract value will be £1,000,000. On the other hand, if Contractor B has four projects being worked on each valued at £500,000, then their maximum contract value would only need to be listed at £500,000. The insurer for Contractor B will pay a maximum of £500,000 for any one claim within the policy period.

How does the economy affect the construction insurance industry?

The insurance industry plays a significant role in the UK economy; UK insurers contributed £29 billion to the economy in 2015. The construction industry will play a large part in this, although it is difficult to put forward an exact figure. The premiums can have a large variation because they are based on a number of factors, including activities undertaken, height and depth limits worked to, the use of heat on site, if there is any work with asbestos, number of employees, payroll, turnover and locations worked at. The claims experience will play a significant part in the underwriter process.

We've looked at the insurance industry and the contribution to the economy. Let's take a look at the role of the construction industry. In 2014 the construction industry accounted for £105 billion in the economic output, with 2.1 million jobs or 6.2% of the UK workforce employed in the construction industry. These are companies like any other, affected by the state of the economy. Very often, it is the smaller companies which are the first to suffer when there's an economic downturn. As we saw with the 2007/08 recession, contracts were suspended and this led to certain sites being left half finished. The companies who couldn't find work had to make parts of their workforce redundant. Of course, if these workers are unable to find work with another company, this can lead to an increase in the unemployment rate and potentially the number of people that may be eligible for welfare provided by the state. Not only could this see a decrease in the number of companies, it will likely lead to a decrease in the number of policies these companies require. Very often this can lead to companies taking out the essential insurances only. As a result, a domino effect can occur; the insurance brokers may require fewer staff, the underwriters may be writing fewer policies which in turn could lead to a decrease in their staffing numbers. Not only does the economy affect the construction industry, it also affects the insurance industry as well.

When the economy is stronger, more people are willing to commit to having work carried out, whether this is private home owners looking to make changes to their property, councils looking to regenerate town centres or large housing developers meeting public demand. This leads to general increases in the number of companies and the number of policies required, which will then lead to an increase in the number of workers that will be required along with extra staff at the insurance brokers to administer the policies and lastly an increase in the number of staff at the insurance company.

Declaration verses a non-declaration policy

If we asked to you to project your turnover for the next year, how accurate do you think you would be? Have you considered the number of staff that you would require to meet the business demands and would you be able to project the salaries paid to your staff? These are some of the problems that construction companies face year on year with their insurance. There are two ways that the insurance policy is calculated and based. The first is on a declaration basis; this requires the company to project their figures for the forthcoming year. This includes their payroll, turnover and maximum contract value. Throughout the year the insured will not need to declare each additional employee they take on, and unless they expect to see dramatic increases to the payroll they would not need to declare each increase. At the end of the policy period a declaration form is sent in their renewal pack. This may include the projections for that policy period, a column for their declared figures and another column for the projections for the following year.

An insurer is entitled to charge a declaration premium for any increase to the projected figures. Although this may seem unfair, the insurer will be accepting an increase in the risk and also the chances of a claim coming in. For example, if a company projects their payroll to direct employees at circa £150,000 but declares their payments at £300,000 then the company has benefited from being insured for twice the cover whilst only paying half of the premium to the insurer. The insurer accepted to cover the company based on the projections made at the start of the policy period and may have charged a higher premium if the projected figures reflected the declared figures at the end of the policy period.

If you find yourself being quoted for a declaration policy, it may be worth considering over-projecting at the quote stage. This would give you a buffer in case the company sees increases on the projected figures and may result in a lower declaration charge. For smaller companies where they only carry out a small number of contracts throughout the year, where the turnover has not seen large changes over a number of years and will not be tendering for larger contracts, then a declaration based policy may be the most suitable and cost effective. This is because there can be lower associated costs at the beginning of the policy period.

The second option is a non-declaration based policy and, as previously advised, these account for approximately 5% of the policies in the market. At M&DH we are extremely fortunate to have access to a close working relationship with a group of underwriters who will write non-declaration based policies. The premiums are based on projections like the declaration based policies, although at the end of the policy period the insurers will not charge for the increase to these projected figures irrespective of the increase of the figures one may face. The underwriters will often charge a higher minimum premium than for a policy that is declaration based.

Claims within the sector and how this affects the industry

Ultimately, the reason for having insurance is that in the unfortunate event that one does suffer a loss, the insurance company will pay for the loss incurred. There aren't exact figures for claims in respect of the construction industry alone; however, in 2015 there was a reported £2.9 million paid out for employer's liability claims. If we accept that the construction industry as a whole carries a fair amount of risk, then it would also be fair to say that the majority of these claims may also be associated with this sector. In order to cover the cost of the claims, the premiums paid by each company may need to increase in order to cover the deficit.

This could be attributed to the particular occupation that carries the greatest risk of claims, for example a piling contractor could carry a higher risk of third party property damage claims through vibration damage. If there's an increase in the frequency of the claims more generally, then the underwriters may look to charge an increase to all piling contractors for which they are writing, or they may no longer look to write these types of policies.

By far the biggest contribution to the claims figures will be the fraudulent claims submitted. In 2014 there were almost 130,000 fraudulent insurance claims totalling over £1.3 billion. If these were to be paid out, that is another £1.3 billion which would need to be recovered through increases to all insurance premiums. The insurance industry is like any other business and can only continue to operate in the way that it does by ensuring that fraudulent claims are filtered out to stop unnecessary payments and ensure that the premium charged to the client is a fair reflection of the risk they pose and to make sure that they contribute to the general insurance pot.

To conclude, there are a number of considerations to be made when arranging the insurance for a construction company. Not only do you need to choose what type of cover you require or are required by a contract to have, you also need to decide on what type of broker you wish to be dealing with. It is always recommended to go through a truly independent broker like M&DH Insurance Services Ltd. They are not restricted to only approaching one market or insurer but will carry out a full market exercise to ensure that the policy put forward is the best policy for your company. You can rest assured that you will be dealing with qualified professionals from start to finish throughout your time with us. We will discuss your requirements to ensure that your policy is on the right basis and if necessary put forward a non-declaration policy if this is better suited.

Glossary

Annual Accounts – Financial statements, usually prepared by an accountant on behalf of a business, reflecting performance of the business during a specific financial year.

Annual Investment Allowance (AIA) – Tax relief introduced in 2008 that allows a 100% first year allowance to be claimed against taxable income for capital investment in certain 'plant and machinery' assets during that year. The maximum amount of allowance is limited to £200,000 per year (for tax year 2016/17), meaning that up to £200,000 of the purchase costs can be deducted from the taxable profits of the business.

Association of Certified Chartered Accountants (ACCA) – A leading international accountancy body with over 600,000 members and students in 178 countries.

Auditor – Accountancy firm or practitioner authorised to undertake audit work. Audit work is regulated by the UK accountancy profession, and carried out to ascertain the validity and reliability of financial statements, and to provide independent analysis of internal controls. Businesses with a turnover exceeding £6.5m and all publicly traded companies (plc) must prepare audited accounts.

Capital Expenditure – Funds spent acquiring or upgrading physical assets such as property, industrial machinery or equipment. Assets generally have a long-term use within a business.

Capital Gains Tax (CGT) – Tax charge that arises on the profit made by a person when certain assets are sold, given away, exchanged, or otherwise disposed of, whether in the UK or overseas. Cars and some personal assets disposed of under a certain value, and your principal residence, are exempt. The capital gains tax free annual allowance is currently £11,100 (2016/17). All qualifying gains over this are charged at 10% or 20% (18% or 28%, if residential property), dependent on the individual's total income in the tax year (See Entrepreneurs' Relief).

CIS300 – Monthly CIS return submitted by businesses that operate the CIS, detailing payments made to subcontractors through to the 5th day of the reporting month.

CIS Deduction – A withholding tax deducted from the labour element of payments made to subcontractors. Rate of deduction is 0%, 20% or 30% depending on the subcontractor's payment status with HMRC.

CIS Offset – Method available for companies for offsetting deductions suffered from payments received against ongoing CIS, PAYE or other tax liabilities. Typically forms part of a monthly Employer Payment Summary (EPS).

Companies Act 2006 (CA2006) – Legislation that forms the primary source of UK company law introduced in 2006, and was the longest piece of legislation in parliament history until the Corporation Tax act in 2009. Reformed and replaced the previous Companies Act 1985.

Companies House – An executive agency of the UK Government. Acts as the registrar of companies and deals with all formations, registrations and filing duties, as well as handling any breaches of Companies Act 2006. Information held on registered companies including financial statements and details of shareholders and officers is made readily available to the public domain.

Construction Industry Scheme (CIS) – Regulatory framework that governs payments between contractors and subcontractors in the construction industry.

Construction Industry Training Board (CITB) Levy – Annual contribution made by employers in the construction industry to support skills and training. Actual levy is based on annual wage bill, including labour-only subcontractors.

Corporation Tax – Tax on the taxable profits of limited companies including clubs, societies and associations. For 2016/17, the main rate is 20%.

CT600 – Annual self-assessed tax return submitted by limited companies detailing corporation tax liabilities. Due 12 months after the end of accounting period.

Designated Member – Member of LLP with responsibility for signing and delivering accounts, notifying Companies House of membership changes, and appointing auditors where applicable.

Dividends – Payments made by a company to its shareholders. Paid out of taxed profits.

Employer Payment Summary (EPS) – An electronic report sent by a business operating PAYE and/or CIS to HMRC. It is used to report to HMRC any reduction in the CIS/PAYE payable by a business for a given month, notably when a company has suffered CIS deductions itself and wishes to offset this against what is payable.

Employment Status Indicator (ESI) – Online form that checks the employment status of subcontractors.

Entrepreneurs' Relief – A form of Capital Gains Tax (CGT) relief for the disposal of businesses. First £10 million of a qualifying gain in a lifetime is subject to a reduced CGT of 10%. Excess at normal rates of 10% or 20%.

Financial Year – The period in which an organisation prepares its financial statements.

HM Revenue & Customs (HMRC) – UK government body responsible for indirect taxes (VAT, for example) and direct taxes (corporation tax and income tax). Formed by the merger of HM Customs & Excise and Inland Revenue.

Inheritance Tax (IHT) – Tax paid on an estate when someone dies. Estates under £325,000 are exempt. 40% tax charged over this amount. Additional £175,000 exemption amount is being phased in to cover leaving the family home to your descendants.

Institute of Chartered Accountants in England and Wales (ICAEW) – The largest of the UK professional accountancy organisations. Chartered body operates in the public interest, regulating members, and has representational roles with the government, the EU and other worldwide bodies.

Limited Liability Company (Ltd) – Type of business organisation in which the liability of the shareholders is limited.

Limited Liability Partnership (LLP) – Partnership in which the members have some form of limited liability. Exhibits characteristics common to limited companies and traditional self-employed partnerships.

Making Tax Digital (MTD) – Government initiative bringing about changes to the tax-related reporting system.

Member – Member of an LLP who is not a designated member.

Memorandum & Articles (M&A) – Documents that detail the constitution of a company and govern the relationship the company has with the outside world.

National Insurance Contributions (NICs) – Contributory system that manages entitlement to certain state provided benefits. Comes in six classes: Class 1 paid by employers and employees on earnings; Class 1A paid by employers on certain benefits in kind made available or paid to employees; Class 1B paid by employers who enter into a PAYE settlement agreement; Class 2 paid by self-employed people (due to be abolished from April 2017); Class 3 paid voluntarily by people with gaps in their contribution history and Class 4 paid by self-employed people and based on a percentage of the profit made from their self-employment.

Option to Tax – Voluntarily places a piece of land or building, and any associated construction work, within the scope of VAT. Applied for through HMRC.

Pay As You Earn (PAYE) – System of collecting tax revenue by withholding income tax from employees.

Real Time Information (RTI) – Online payroll submission and payments to subcontractors are made using monthly real time full payment submissions (FPS). Undertaken by payroll software.

Retention – Amount of money often withheld from payments on long-term contracts, which is released upon completion and approval of a contract.

Self-Assessment (SA) – System within the UK tax regime that shifts the burden of administering tax affairs onto an individual (for income tax) or a company (for corporation tax).

Self-Invested Pension Plan (SIPP) – Pension plan that enables the holder to choose investments, although the scheme is administered externally. Offers excellent tax benefits.

Small Self-Administered Scheme (SSAS) – Flexible pension scheme operated and fund managed by business owners, rather than external administrators. Offers excellent tax benefits.

Sole Trader – Type of business entity where there is no legal distinction between the owner and the business. The owner receives all of the profits, and is liable for all of the debts.

Tax Year – In the UK the fiscal tax year runs from 6th April to 5th April for individuals. For most limited companies the tax year follows the financial year that the company uses to prepare its annual accounts.

Unique Tax Reference (UTR) – Unique ten-digit number issued by HMRC to self-employed individuals, partnerships, limited companies and limited liability partnerships. The UTR is used in conjunction with all taxation matters.

Valuation – Regular survey and valuation of ongoing construction work under certain contracts which form the basis of regular interim payments to subcontractors carrying out the work.

Value Added Tax (VAT) – An indirect tax that is a form of consumption tax; a tax on spending and services. In the UK, the standard VAT rate is 20% and is applied to almost all goods or services that a business may provide. Some construction services may not attract 20% VAT, instead falling into 0% band (housing new builds) or a reduced 5% band (listed buildings and some residential conversions).

About the authors

Jeffrey Lermer

Jeffrey Lermer took his degree in Business Economics at Southampton University in 1985. He augmented a strong financial proficiency by qualifying as a Chartered Accountant in 1988 with Stoy Hayward (BDO), joined Sobell Rhodes in 1992, became a partner at 29 and left aged 38 to set up his own practice in 2003.

In 1993, Jeffrey acquired his first construction client and loved the no-nonsense and straight-talking approach of clients in this industry. You always know where you stand: if a contractor is not happy, they will tell you! Also, dealing with professionals is part of the contractor's day job, so they are used to it.

At JLA, Jeffrey is called on to provide guidance and advice on business profits, taxation and structures. He is a Fellow of the ICAEW, Tax Committee member of the Association of Certified Chartered Accountants (ACCA), a regular speaker at the ACCA budget breakfast, member of the Construction Industry Reform Implementation Panel and a member of their Tax Faculty. Jeffrey is an expert on trust and estate planning issues and the construction industry, and works closely with his clients' own personal investment advisors.

Over the years, Jeffrey has built up a large client portfolio of businesses and individuals, providing leading-edge general practice and tax consultancy. He enjoys strong client relationships that go beyond the boundaries of traditional accountancy – often assuming the role of a client's financial director. This unique and privileged status affords Jeffrey the platform to provide pro-active, hands-on commercial advice and more importantly, provides him with the satisfaction of watching his clients' businesses evolve and expand.

Jeffrey regularly lectures and advises businesses and associations on a wide variety of tax-related topics including, 'Inheritance Tax for the Elderly', 'Optimal Remuneration Structure', 'Offshore Management' and 'Property, Construction, Development and Selling'.

Both a lateral thinker and natural communicator, Jeffrey enjoys the intricacies of financial planning, particularly focusing on minimising taxation liabilities and maximising investment returns. His economic solutions are not only well received for their financial implications, but also, to his credit, because highly complex information is conveyed in simple English.

Jeffrey is 52 and married to Lucy, an office manager for a Member of Parliament in the House of Commons. They have four daughters. He attains personal satisfaction through continued improvement of his religious education at the local synagogue.

www.linkedin.com/pub/jeffrey-lermer/14/842/460

Email jeff@lermer.co.uk

Telephone 020 8441 1140

Karen Wyrwas

Karen loves to work with people and numbers in equal measure. Her first career was in computer science and after gaining her degree at the University of Manchester, she enjoyed ten years working in this field, mainly developing whizzy graphics and computer-aided design software, in both the UK and Australia. She then took some time out to raise a family, after which she found herself looking for a new challenge. People and numbers… numbers and people… What better than a new vocation in accountancy? And she hasn't looked back! She loves getting involved in her clients' businesses and using her problem-solving skills to ensure every business is optimally set up for tax.

Karen joined JLA in its early days and immediately took to the firm's strong ethos for pro-active advice, rather than purely crunching the numbers. This attracts a wide variety of clients, including JLA's solid core of construction clients. She takes great pleasure in navigating clients through the accountancy minefield to structure and grow their businesses, enabling them to achieve their financial goals.

Now the firm's Tax Manager, Karen enjoys the annual challenge of digesting the latest Budget changes and helping JLA's clients understand and plan for new legislation.

When not perusing HMRC's latest missive, Karen has a passion for watching all kinds of sport, especially if her children are competing!

Email karen@lermer.co.uk

Telephone 020 8344 2971

Laurence Cobb

Laurence is a member of the Society of Construction Law, writes articles for the construction press and lectures to industry bodies and clients. He is referred to as an expert in both Chambers and Legal 500 Directories. He was educated at King Edward VII School, Lytham, Manchester University and Chester Law College.

Laurence is a partner and International Head of Construction & Engineering at Taylor Wessing. He specialises in construction and engineering law; with considerable experience in dealing with dispute management for all forms of projects, ranging from traditional building contracts to complex infrastructure schemes, both national and international. Laurence advises clients in mediation, litigation, adjudication, arbitration and expert determination, as well as during negotiated settlements and in meeting pre-action requirements.

Email l.cobb@taylorwessing.com

Telephone 020 7300 4918